Practical Band Instrument
Repair Manual

Practical Band Instrument
Repair Manual

Clayton H. Tiede

Mankato State University

Third Edition

WM. C. BROWN COMPANY PUBLISHERS
Dubuque, Iowa

Consulting Editor
Fred Westphal
California State University, Sacramento

Printed in the United States of America

To my wife Eunice

CONTENTS

Contents

LIST OF PLATES

PREFACE

This book is the culmination of concern for the band director's instrument repair problems and was written in response to numerous requests from directors, instrumentalists, students, and others in the field of music and music education.

A small percentage of the band directors teaching today are fortunate enough to be located in a city which has music instrument repair facilities. This advantage, however, does not relieve the director of the responsibility to instruct his students in the proper care of their own instruments, or those of the school, nor does it eliminate his repair problems or guarantee immediate help in cases of emergency. The instruction for the proper care of the musical instrument, the skill required for the handling of emergency repairs, and the knowledge to prevent certain major repairs still rest on the shoulders of the band director and are solely his responsibility.

The band director located in a small community which has no facilities for instrument repair is faced with the same responsibilities and problems. His obligations, however, are augmented by the fact that he must see that instruments are transported to and from a city where a repair shop is located. The fact that the director must do this on his own time is in itself a slight irritation; the biggest headache is what to do about the student who is deprived of his instrument. The student may sit idle for a week or weeks; obviously his instruction suffers and at the same time the band is deprived of an instrument which often can be a lone, vital instrument or one belonging to a first-chair player. In these cases the wait for repairs is even more disastrous.

If the repair is a major one, the wait is necessary and tolerable. Many times, however, because the director and/or the student have not been trained to notice the need for minor repairs until they develop into major ones, or because they have not been instructed in the care and maintenance of the instrument, these major repair jobs are the result of neglect.

On the other hand, and equally as often, repairs sent to a repair shop are of the simplest nature and could have been handled easily by the band director or a student with a modicum of knowledge and instruction in this type of work.

Considering the present "energy crisis," the possibility of a severe reduction in the regular service calls made by the local music stores or the inability of the director to provide transportation may well force an increased need for preventive maintenance and "home" repairs.

These all point up the fact that the band director has a sizable and continual problem which can be greatly minimized with a little knowledge and a few basic tools.

It is this lack of knowledge so prevalent in the training of the music educator, primarily band, of the past and present that has given purpose to this manual. Few educational institutions in the United States offer such a course as part of the band director's training. It is gratifying, however, to learn that several summer music camps are including such a course in their program and more are following suit each year. Even more enlightening is the knowledge that some colleges and universities are recognizing this need for instruction and are adding instrument repair courses to their curricula. Add to this the emphasis by instrument manufacturers and we have a small awakening to an old and irritating problem.

In the course of writing this book I have talked with many band directors, music supervisors, and administrators. Most of their opinions of the text have been very favorable. There have been, however, two points of opposition. These are that the director does not have the time to do the work and that the cost of tools would be better spent for additional instruments.

The time factor is not a valid objection. Most of the repairs outlined in this manual can be completed in less time than it would take the director to deliver the instrument to a repair shop. The objection to the expense involved likewise is invalid. Two broken drumheads or one major repair job would almost buy the tools and materials outlined in this text. Furthermore the money saved with proper care and maintenance of instruments and on minor repairs will buy many additional instruments over a period of time.

It is true that there are pamphlets and books on instrument repair and maintenance; however, there are only a few of these. Then too, they are either technical manuals far too advanced and detailed for the average director or student, or they are simple little booklets offering a minimal amount of advice on how to care for an instrument with little, if any, instruction given to perform even the most minor repair jobs.

This book is an attempt to provide all the information contained in the pamphlets on the care of the instruments, as well as to condense and simplify the instructions in the technical manuals on repair and maintenance.

All repair operations contained in the book have been clearly outlined with illustrations, photographs, and step-by-step procedures enabling the band director, layman, or student to complete them with a minimal amount of technique, tools, or training. Should the suggestion be made in the text to send the problem to a professional repairman, please realize that correct terminology should be used in the explanation of work to be done and in the description of the parts, pieces, and/or sections of the instrument to be considered. Also an understanding of what is involved, what should be expected, and what is meant by such terms as "overhaul," "playing condition," and "regulate" is helpful.*

In addition to a "General Care" section which relates to the basic repair and maintenance common to a family of instruments, separate chapters deal with specific instruments, or those of similar structure, and discuss the following:

1. A drawing which labels the various parts of the instrument.
2. A list of specific tools, accessories, and equipment needed for maintenance and minor repairs.
3. General instruction, rules, and precautions for assembling and handling the instrument.
4. Step-by-step procedures, with illustrations, for any and all repair work discussed.
5. Notes, special tips, and suggestions for the general care and cleaning of the instrument.
6. An "Instrument Inspection Check Sheet" to be used for periodic checking.
7. A "Class Project Sheet" to be used for course work.

*See Appendix E for sample repair brochures and descriptions.

The material in the text is organized so that it can be used as a reference-instruction manual for anyone wishing to do his own repairs; or it can be used as a textbook for instrument repair courses. It should not, however, be thought of as a manual for the training of a professional repairman.

Specifically the text will aid the band director or anyone in the music profession in the following ways.

1. Enable the individual to handle his own minor or emergency repairs.
2. Offer instruction and information on how to prevent, to a certain extent, the need for major repairs.
3. Provide, for the band director, a source with which he can teach reliable students, with a certain degree of mechanical ability, to handle the inspection, maintenance, and repair of the band instruments.
4. Enable the musician to learn how better to care for his own instrument.
5. Serve as a text for courses in instrument repair and maintenance.

These five main factors enable the band director to turn lost time into valuable teaching hours, cut down repair costs in the music budget, and, by improving the playing condition and life of the instruments, raise performance standards and speed the advancement of his students.

INSTRUMENT INSPECTION CHECK SHEETS

At the close of each chapter is an Instrument Inspection Check Sheet. These sheets can be duplicated and, when filled out, provide the music director with an inventory as well as a complete report on the condition of the students' instruments as well as those of the school.

The reports can be handled in two ways. They can be filled out and turned in by each student as a report and spot check of his own instrument; or the job of inspecting all the instruments can be delegated to one or more persons, the forms filled out and signed, and turned in to the director.

If possible the report should contain information as to how the instrument plays. Remarks of this nature can be written under "Other Comments" at the bottom of the sheet.

CLASS PROJECT SHEETS

At the close of each chapter there is also a Class Project Sheet which can be used by the individual for self-evaluation or by an instructor teaching a course in band instrument repair maintenance.

The Project Sheets provide a chapter-by-chapter evaluation of the individual or student and his ability to perform the prescribed emergency and permanent repairs, and to demonstrate the proper handling, care, and attention which should be given the wind and percussion instruments.

INTRODUCTION

One of the major causes for repair bills is the damage resulting from the lack of proper cleaning and the control of moisture. If an instrumental director can only advise and instruct his students in this one phase of preventive maintenance, he has contributed immensely to their efforts of achieving competent technical skills and lasting musical rewards.

Moisture in brass instruments causes a chemical reaction called oxidation which either rusts or corrodes the metal. In the woodwind instruments, it can cause the wood to swell and crack, metal rods to rust and bind, and pads to rot. Minimizing the effects of moisture can add years of life to the instrument. Moisture can come from the breath and condense on the inside of the instrument, from atmospheric changes, or from a direct source such as saliva. Saliva from the human body contains carbonic acid which is present at all times. Other acids are formed in the mouth, depending on what is eaten or drunk. This fact alone should be enough to discourage anyone from chewing gum, eating candy, or drinking soft drinks just before playing. Rinsing the mouth out with water will lessen the amount of acids in the saliva.

Acids attack brass and act more rapidly on parts that have been soft-soldered, such as joints, water key nipples, and tone holes, and can even eat into clarinet and saxophone pads. Acids also have the ability to weld two movable sections together, such as valve caps and tuning slides. Care should always be taken to remove as much moisture as possible from an instrument before it is stored for any length of time. Well-greased slides and oiled valves will resist moisture and prevent oxidation.

Acids from the saliva are not alone the chief danger in connection with moisture. Spring water and natural well water contain certain elements such as magnesium, calcium, calcium carbonates, sulphates, potassium, and some amounts of chlorides of sodium which, when combined, produce certain salt solutions. Hard water has a high content of these salts which, when dried out, leave a white, gritty substance on the metal or pad. When the water on a moving part of the instrument undergoes this process, as on valves or slides, the abrasive residue wears away the thin coatings of chrome or nickel. When water is used in place of oil, distilled water should be used and cleaning the inside of the instrument should be done regularly.

The collection of foreign matter is not only a sanitation hazard, but can seriously impair the intonation of the instrument. This is especially true with woodwinds. Many times dirt or foreign particles will cause the throat tones of a clarinet to speak poorly or an oboe to fail to overblow its octaves properly. This dirt is also blown through the instrument and gets into the working mechanism. Take for instance a trombone slide which has a clearance between the inside slide and the outside slide of approximately .003 in., or about the thickness of a human hair. It is quite easy to see the results if dirt or other foreign matter are blown into this area; the action is impaired and metal is ground away by friction. Systematic cleaning of an instrument should always be undertaken to remove lipstick, food particles, dirt, tobacco, and the ever-present "saliva mold" that collect.

So far we have touched only on the deterioration of the instrument from within. Corrosion or oxidation can occur on the outside as well. This comes chiefly from acids left by perspiration. Most perspiration contains lactic, butyric, and small amounts of hydrochloric acids while others contain an alkaline solution, all of which will attack metal. It is not uncommon to find valve casings, mouthpipes, tubing, or braces eaten through from the acids in the perspiration left by the hand. If one does not use a guard of some kind (such as commonly used around cornet valves), care should be taken to wipe the instrument clean after each use.

In cleaning the outside of the instrument, realize that all (with few exceptions) brass instruments have a lacquer finish. For this reason, the instrument must never be submerged in hot water nor should any cleaner be used that has an abrasive quality or a strong chemical agent that will discolor or dissolve the lacquer. To prevent damage to the finish, only those cleaners specifically designated for lacquered instruments should be used.

To clean the finish on a silver- or gold-plated instrument, avoid those products which have a "gritty" composition. This is an abrasive agent that will wear the precious metal away. There are some good quality silver polishes on the market which may be used. However, most repairmen use a paste of "whiting powder"* and alcohol. Plain whiting powder on a cloth will also work well.

Carrying cases: A strong, sturdy, well-blocked and padded instrument case is one of the cheapest insurance policies a musician can have against plaguing repair bills. A cheaply built case is often more dangerous than no case at all because when they are thrown into lockers, cages, buses, or storage rooms, there is a false feeling of security that the instrument is adequately protected.

Equally as dangerous is the case which has broken hinges, locks, or handles which can fall apart at a moment's notice and cause severe damage to the instrument inside.

Concern must also be given to the padding, straps, and locks within the case. Little protection is afforded the instrument if it is allowed to rattle around inside the case and be knocked and banged against the blocks or other hard unprotected sides and corners. The instrument must fit snugly into the cushioned lining and be held firmly by leather straps or covered locks. Loose articles such as bottles of oil, reed caps, mouthpieces, cork grease, reed clips, and lyres should be kept in a separate compartment and locked so they cannot fall out. Even the mouthpiece, if it does not have a separate special compartment or "tiedown" area, should be protected by placing it in a small cardboard box or clean wool sock.

Needless to say, the instrument case is not a substitute suitcase, briefcase, or gym bag. Extra music books, bag lunches, and gym clothes stuffed into an already compact instrument case can cause damage to slides, valves, keys, and pads.

One final word of caution is to be certain that rubber bands or pencil erasers are kept out of the case. These have a sulphur content in them that can quickly tarnish gold or silver.

*Whiting powder can be purchased at a drugstore.

Practical Band Instrument
Repair Manual

unit one

BRASS INSTRUMENTS

Chapter 1

GENERAL CARE

In spite of the numerous times that brass players are reminded of cleaning their instrument, the lack of care remains one of the major causes for brass instruments being sent to a repair shop. Moisture, usually saliva, in brass instruments causes a chemical reaction called oxidation which either rusts or corrodes the metal. Most oxidation can be attributed to a process called "electrolytic corrosion" which accelerates the action of the acids produced by bacteria when two dissimilar (silver and brass) metals are in contact with one another (silver mouthpiece and brass receiver). The most damaging result of this chemical reaction occurs in the area of the mouthpipe. If left unattended, small pink spots will appear on the outside of the tubing. These are not caused by an acid from the hands eating from the outside in through the pipe, but rather from saliva acids eating (through the metal) from the inside out. This chemical reaction, if unchecked, will continue until a sizeable hole develops. True, these can be patched, but the damage has already been done to the inside smooth bore of the mouthpipe. In short, this major cause of repair can be lessened and even eliminated by always removing the mouthpiece from the instrument when it is not being played, by periodically cleaning both the mouthpiece and mouthpipe with lukewarm water and a mild soap, and then, when the mouthpipe is dry, applying a thin film of valve or key oil to the bore. A systematic schedule of cleaning and oiling valves, slides, springs, and mouthpiece coupled with a quick rundown of the respective "Instrument Inspection Check Sheet" at the conclusion of each chapter will greatly minimize the need for repairs and enhance the playing ability of the instrument.

TOOLS AND ACCESSORIES FOR THE REPAIR AND MAINTENANCE OF THE BRASS INSTRUMENTS[1]

BASIC

TOOLS

Small rawhide mallet
Pair of ordinary pliers
Pair of roundnose pliers
Pair of wire cutter pliers
Razor blades (single edge)
Flexible brush
Mouthpiece brushes
Nail or center punches
Mouthpiece puller

ACCESSORIES

Penetrating oil
Petroleum jelly
Steel wool (fine)

SPECIFIC

Piston Valve Instruments

TOOLS

Valve cleaning rod

ACCESSORIES

Valve oil
Three sets of bottom valve springs (one each for cornet/trumpet, baritone, and bass horn)
Assorted valve stem felts for above instruments
Several strips of clean cloth
Several tubes of water key cork (3/8" dia.) and one dozen precut corks
Two tubes of valve stem cork, one for the cornet and one for the bass horn. (This is sufficient to handle all the valve instruments.)
One dozen each (cornet and bass) "valve button felts"

Trombone

TOOLS

Trombone cleaning rod
Bumper remover

ACCESSORIES

Slide oil
Several long strips of cloth
One sheet of 3/32" cork

Rotary Valve Instruments

TOOLS

Screwdriver (wide 1/4" to 3/8") with thin-tipped blade

1. See Appendix C for supply companies that will provide catalogs.

ACCESSORIES

Key oil
Several strips of clean cloth
Several sticks of French horn bumper cork or neo-
prene rubber
Several feet of braided, 30-lb. test fishline
Large wooden thread spool

I. THE MOUTHPIECE

A. Stuck Mouthpiece

The most common and most frequent repair is the stuck mouthpiece. This is caused by leaving the mouthpiece in the horn when it is put away where, because of the action of saliva acids, it becomes "frozen." It can also be caused by the incorrect placement of the mouthpiece into the horn. Many students place the mouthpiece into the instrument and then give it a whack with the palm of their hand. This forces the mouthpiece into the horn beyond its normal placement. Correct placement of the mouthpiece into the instrument consists of placing it into the ferrule and then giving it a slight clockwise twist as if it were being screwed in. When it is to be removed it is then "unscrewed." If, as will sometimes happen, one does become stuck, some procedures to remove it follow.

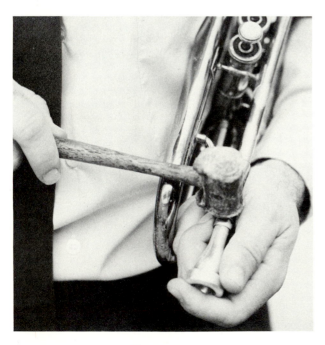

Figure 1.1

Materials needed:

1. Small rawhide mallet
2. Mouthpiece puller

Procedure:

1. Grasp the instrument securely under one arm, making sure the braces and tubing in the immediate area are well supported. With one hand pull on the mouthpiece with a twisting motion while with the other hand tap on the ferrule, or mouthpiece receiver, with a rawhide mallet.

CAUTION: When working with the trombone, (1) be certain slides are locked and (2) strike on the mouthpiece receiver, NOT on the cork barrel.

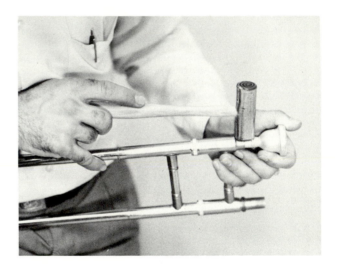

Figure 1.2

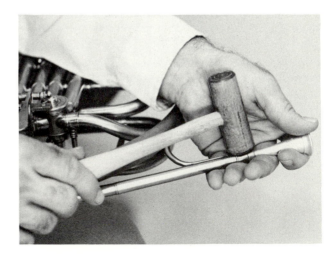

Figure 1.3

A band director who is frequently faced with this problem should buy a mouthpiece puller of which there are several good ones on the market. The ones pictured (Figs. 1.4 and 1.5) are the Thompson and the "Pep" mouthpiece pullers. The Thompson contains a set of 11 collars graduated in size. To use this tool simply select the correct size set of collars that fit the mouthpiece next to the ferrule. Place the instrument into the jig as pictured and, by unscrewing the jaws, remove the mouthpiece. The Pep employs the use of three small rods which are screwed in or out to fit tightly against the mouthpiece next

Figure 1.4

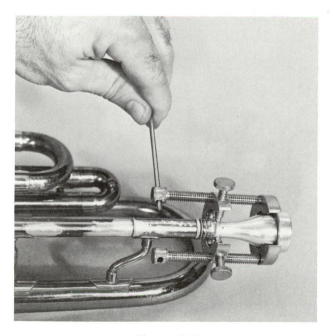

Figure 1.5

to the ferrule. This puller, though more compact than most, provides only three small places of contact and, if the mouthpiece is badly stuck, can gouge the rim of the ferrule.[1]

After it has been removed, care must be given the mouthpiece itself. When it has been forced into the ferrule and removed by force, it will have acquired ridges or minute burrs on the shank. These must and can be removed by soaking in vinegar, or by rubbing lightly with steel wool, emery paper, or baking soda. If steel wool or emery paper are used, caution must be taken so as not to remove any of the silver plating.

B. Cleaning the Mouthpiece

A dirty mouthpiece is a sanitation hazard and can impair the intonation of the instrument. A mouthpiece filled with "mold" is similar to a small bore mouthpiece and, although the player will suddenly be able to play high notes, his middle and low range will suffer considerably.

If the "mold" within the mouthpiece is quite thick and hard, it can be softened and removed by soaking it in vinegar for half an hour or so. It may then be brushed loose and flushed away.

Mouthpiece brushes can be bought quite inexpensively; but, if these are not handy, a cleaning brush for an electric razor is good or even a pipe cleaner doubled up. These devices used with warm soapy water will add life to the mouthpiece and performance ability to the player.

C. Straightening the Mouthpiece

The difficulty with an instrument that has intonation problems or is hard to blow can be credited to a mouthpiece with a bent shank. This can be straight-

BENT MOUTHPIECE SHANK

Figure 1.6

1. Although the Thompson is recommended, other mouthpiece pullers are on the market and can be examined through catalogs supplied by dealers (see Appendix C).

ened by taking a pair of roundnose pliers and rotating them inside the shank. Too much pressure should not be applied as it may flange the shank.

The proper tool for reforming the bent shank is a mouthpiece mandrel or Polishing Arbor. However, as effective, less expensive, and more easily attainable is the common center, or nail, punch. Several different sizes can be kept on hand to straighten the bent mouthpiece shanks.

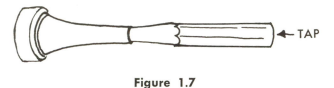

Figure 1.7

A pair of roundnose pliers may also be used in an emergency. In either case too much pressure should not be applied as it may flange the small end of the shank.

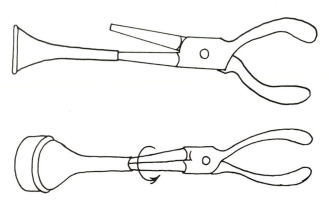

STRAIGHTEN WITH ROUNDNOSE PLIERS

Figure 1.8

One last reminder before leaving the topic of the mouthpiece is to keep it well plated at all times. Gold or silver is the most common plating. Some mouthpieces are plated with nickel, but because of its slipperiness it is not preferred. If the brass works through the plating and comes in contact with an open sore or crack in the lip, serious infection can result.

II. THE TUNING SLIDES

A. Stuck Slides

The second most common problem with brass instruments (primarily piston and rotary) is stuck

slides. If the individual attempts to pull them, extreme care, caution, and common sense must be used. The first step is to look for bends or dents which may be causing the slide to stick, and for any broken or unsoldered joints which would be greatly damaged in the process of attempting to pull the slide. If any of these are found it is best to take the horn to a competent repairman.

The tuning slide is the one we are most concerned with, and although the following discourse deals primarily with it, all procedures and instructions can be applied to any stuck slide. In removing a stuck slide, the procedure is this:

Materials needed:
1. Cloth
2. Rawhide mallet
3. Penetrating oil
4. Drumstick
5. Slide lubricant
6. Fine emery paper or steel wool
7. Petroleum jelly

Procedure: (Removing, cleaning, and replacing)
1. Leave all valves and other slides in to lessen the chances of springing a valve casing or tubing.
2. Grasp the instrument firmly and securely under the arm, and use the hand to reinforce the braces and tubing close to the stuck slide.
3. Wrap a wide cloth or handkerchief around the crook or brace of the stuck slide, leaving enough loose so as to grasp it with the other hand (see Figs. 1.9 and 1.10).

Figure 1.9

Figure 1.10

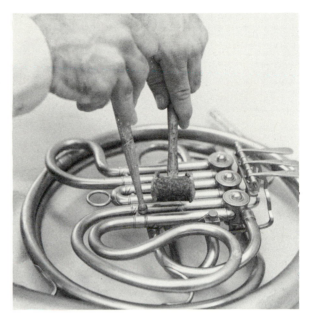

Figure 1.11

4. While holding the instrument secure with the arm and one hand, give a series of firm jerks.
5. If the slide does not come out, tap gently on the tubing in which the slide is stuck to jar loose any "frozen" areas—then repeat the process of jerking. Better still, have someone else do the tapping as you pull.

NOTE: When working with the smaller slides of the piston valve instruments or with the small valve slides of the French horn, an excellent tool is a snare drumstick. The ball end of the stick is placed in the crook of the slide, or with the French horn, behind the slide brace, and tapped to force the slide out (see Fig. 1.11).

6. If the slide remains frozen, apply some penetrating oil to the tubing and let it stand overnight then repeat the foregoing procedure. Heat can be applied to the frozen area by holding it over an alcohol burner. This adds greatly to the effectiveness of the penetrating oil but is dangerous to the finish of a lacquered instrument; for this reason extreme caution must be observed. If neither of these works, it is best to take the instrument to a professional repairman.

NOTE: In discussing the tuning slide on the trombone, consideration here concerns only the bell tuning slide and, on the bass trombone, the second small slide used to tune the instrument when it is in the key of "F."

When removing or replacing the bell tuning slide, care should be used so that there is even pressure on both sides of the slide. If there is an uneven pressure the slide will "cock" and become stuck.

In removing or pushing the slide out, the hands should be placed in between the bell brace and the tuning slide brace and then, using the thumbs against the balancer, the slide should be forced out (see Fig. 1.12).

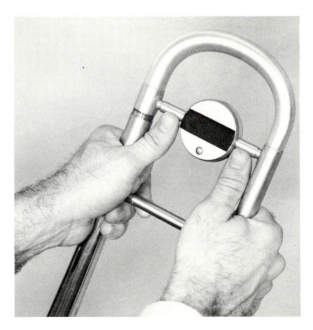

Figure 1.12

In replacing the slide or pushing it in, the thumbs should be hooked under the bell brace and the fingers extended evenly up over the balancer (see Fig. 1.13).

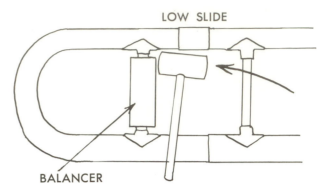

Figure 1.14

8. When replacing the slide, put in only one side at a time and work it in and out until all heavy friction is gone. When both slides work freely in the tubing, wipe them clean of old grease, regrease, and replace the slide.

III. WATER KEYS

Assorted sizes of precut water key (spit valve) corks can be purchased from a local repairman or supply house. The procedure to replace a water key cork is as follows.

Procedure:

1. No glue or cement is used to hold the cork in. Cement or glue becomes hard and brittle when it dries and when a water key is snapped shut the blow can crack the cement and break its holding power. Select a cork, therefore, that is slightly oversized and force it into the cup.

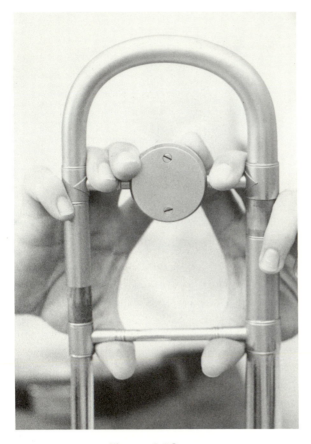

Figure 1.13

If a slide becomes cocked or stuck, no attempt should be made to force the high side in; all effort should be to work the low side out. This can be done by tapping gently with a rawhide mallet on the brace on the side of the slide that is low (farthest in).

7. When any stuck slide is finally removed, be sure to clean the corrosion from the slide-tubing by submerging it in vinegar for half an hour or so and then flushing it with clear water. If this does not remove the scaley matter, it may be rubbed lightly with steel wool or emery paper. Caution must be taken however, so as not to remove any of the metal. The slide should then be wiped clean and greased with plain petroleum jelly or one of the new slide lubricants now on the market.

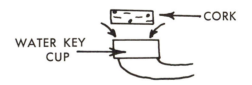

Figure 1.15

2. Press the key down firmly against the rim of the hole (nipple) to assure a good seat.

3. Test the seating of the cork by placing the thumb over the end of one tube of the slide and by blowing through the other. If it leaks, either shift the cork or replace it with another and again test it to make sure it does not leak. If it is impossible

to acquire a selection of precut water key corks, round sticks of cork may be purchased and used in the following manner:

a. Select a cork stick of which the diameter is slightly larger than that of the water key cup.

b. Fit one end of the stick into the cup; as before no cement is used.

c. Use a sharp razor blade and slice off the amount desired.

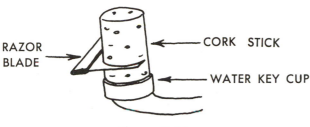

Figure 1.16

d. Check to make sure that the face of the cork in the cup has no heavy grains exposed which can cause a serious leak. If this is the case, either slice off a thin layer of the cork in the cup or replace it entirely.

If the cork, either precut or from a tube, is seating in back but not in front, slice off thin layers until it lies flat against the rim of the hole. If it is seating in front but not in the back, the cork is too thin and must be replaced.

If for some reason the water key has been removed from the crook of a trombone slide the replacing of it can be a real problem. This can be alleviated if two pencils, with erasers, are stuck into the ends of the wire spring that protrudes from the water key. This will provide handles with which to work the water key back into place.

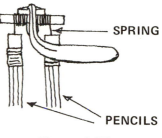

Figure 1.17

Excluding a few experimental models, there are no water keys on the French horn, yet the water that normally collects in the instrument must be removed. For this reason it is important to keep all slides working freely and easily. Water can be removed from the horn in two ways. One is to rotate the horn so the water drains out the mouthpipe. The other is to remove each slide and dump out the water.[1] If a slide cannot be removed, you have a collecting point for saliva which will ruin the tone and corrode the instrument.

1. Double horns especially have a "water slide" for the removal of water. This will affect the tuning, but is not used for such a purpose and must always be left pushed all the way in.

Chapter 2

PISTON VALVE INSTRUMENTS

I. CLEANING AND LUBRICATION

During this process an inspection should be made of parts and sections of the instrument to see that they are in good working condition and operating properly. If repairs are imminent, refer to the respective topics within the chapter.

Materials needed:

1. Flexible brush
2. Valve cleaning rod
3. Valve oil
4. Petroleum jelly
5. Several clean rags
6. Castile soap or a mild detergent

Procedure: (Disassembling and cleaning)

1. Have a basin or sink of lukewarm, sudsy water. For the larger instruments the bathtub works very nicely.

    CAUTION: Do not use hot water, as this will cause the lacquer to peel on a brass instrument. Even some silver instruments have lacquer on them, specifically on the bell. Many strong laundry soaps have the same effect: it is best, therefore, to use a castile soap or a very mild detergent.

2. Unscrew the top valve caps and take out the valves. Pay special attention to the numbers on the valves as you remove them from the casings—*keep them in order!*
3. Using a clean cloth, wipe the old oil off the valves and lay them in order on a clean cloth in a safe place.
4. If the valves are not the spring-barrel type (Plates IV and VI), remove the springs next by unscrewing the bottom valve caps. Wipe off the old grease on the springs and keep them in order by placing them next to their corresponding valve. Wipe out the bottom valve caps also.
5. Next, pull all slides and wipe off the old grease.

6. Submerge the body of the instrument in the warm water and allow it to soak for about ten to fifteen minutes. While the horn is soaking, dip the slides in the water and run the flexible brush through them. Repeat this process until all foreign matter is removed from the inside of the slide tubings. Flush the slides with clean water and dry them.
7. After the slides are wiped dry and put aside, take the body of the horn and repeat the same process as with the slides. Run the flexible brush through all the tubings and flush with clean water.
8. Wipe the horn dry.

Procedure: (Greasing, oiling, and assembling)

1. Take the valve cleaning rod and wrap a clean cloth around it. Do this by inserting one corner of the cloth through the eye of the rod then twisting the rod so as to wind the cloth around it. Be sure to cover the rod entirely with the cloth, even the eye of the rod.
2. Run the rod in and out of the valve casings to remove any last bit of grime or water. The rod may also be used to swab out the tubing, at least as far as it will reach.

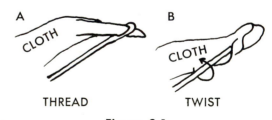

Figure 2.1

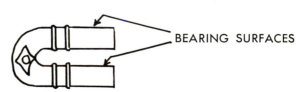

Figure 2.2

3. Before replacing the slides, coat the bearing surfaces with a thin coat of petroleum jelly.
4. Next take the bottom valve caps and coat the inside threads with a thin coat of petroleum jelly before replacing.
5. The springs can also then be given a *very thin* coat of grease and dropped into the casings.
6. Before replacing the valves, wipe them clean, including the ports, and put on three or four drops of good valve oil. For outdoor parades or concerts, use more oil than usual to protect the valves from additional dust and dirt. (Be certain to clean the instrument immediately after such a performance.) It is also a good idea to smear a little petroleum jelly on the threads of the top valve caps.

NOTE: To prevent acids from forming on the inside of the mouthpipe, a few drops of oil can be placed in the mouthpipe. The instrument is then tilted and rotated so the oil will spread evenly in the tube as it flows through. This procedure is also recommended for breaking in a new instrument.

A technique which sounds rather precarious, but is really quite simple and extremely effective in applying oil to the bore of a trumpet or cornet, is to tear off a small piece of kitchen sponge (about one-half inch in diameter) and coat it with oil. Place this in the end of the mouthpipe, depress all valves, and *blow!* The oiled sponge will, with surprising speed, travel through all of the tubing and fly out of the bell end. Several repetitions of this procedure will leave a thin film of oil on the inner surface of the tubing throughout the entire instrument, thus providing an effective deterrent to the oxidation process.

CAUTION:

1. Do not attempt on larger instruments.
2. Do not attempt unless you have a strong set of lungs to send a good blast of air through the instrument.
3. Do not attempt unless you have the expertise to completely disassemble your instrument should the sponge fail to go completely through the instrument on the first try.

PLATE I CORNET

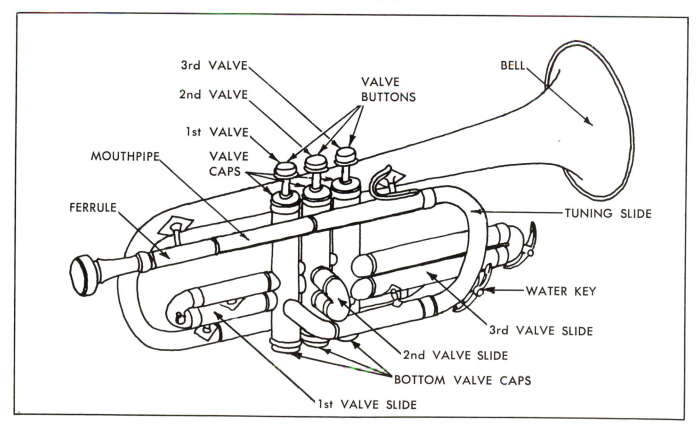

PLATE II—MELLOPHONIUM

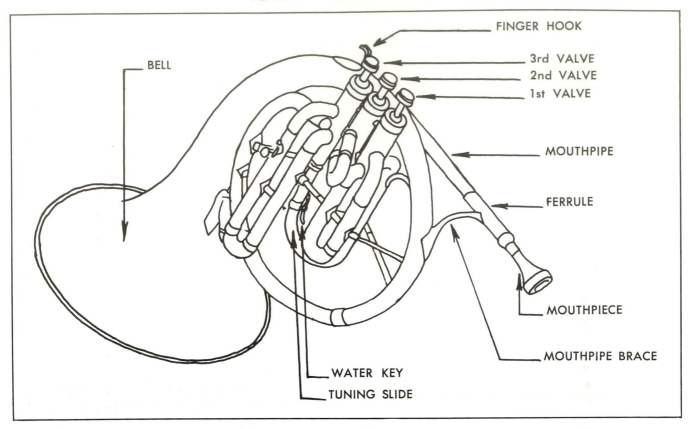

FINGER HOOK

3rd VALVE

2nd VALVE

1st VALVE

BELL

MOUTHPIPE

FERRULE

MOUTHPIECE

MOUTHPIPE BRACE

WATER KEY

TUNING SLIDE

BARITONE HORN

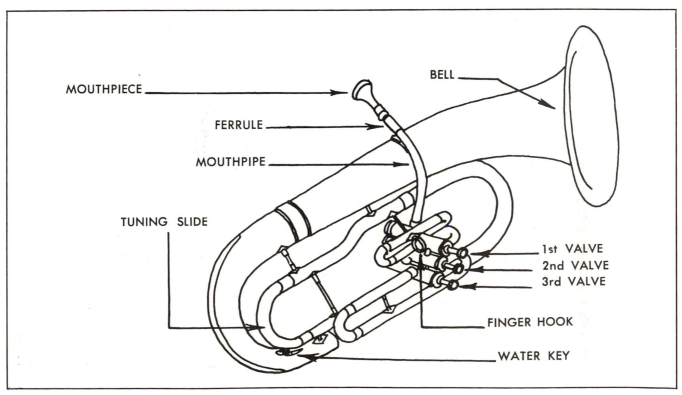

MOUTHPIECE

BELL

FERRULE

MOUTHPIPE

TUNING SLIDE

1st VALVE

2nd VALVE

3rd VALVE

FINGER HOOK

WATER KEY

PLATE III—SOUSAPHONE

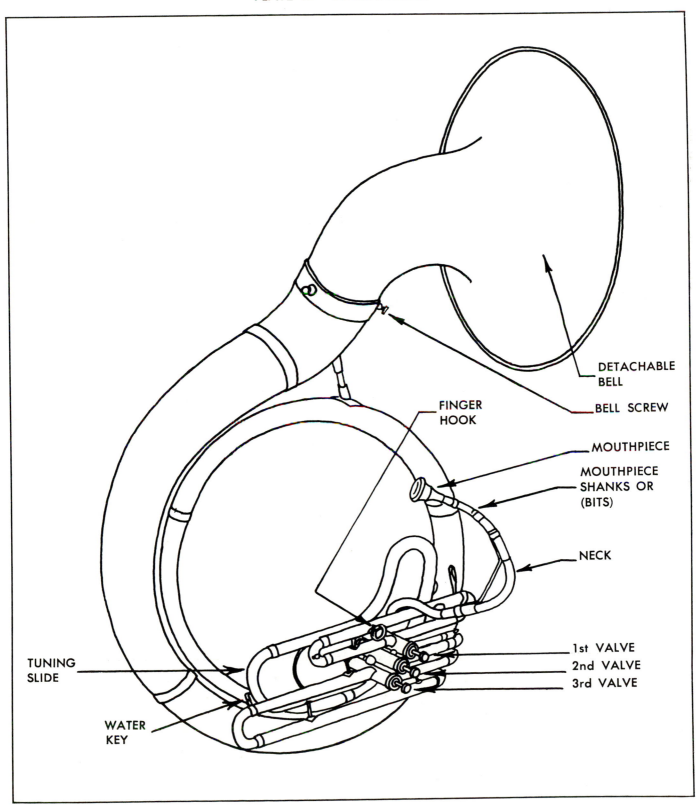

DETACHABLE
BELL

BELL SCREW

MOUTHPIECE

MOUTHPIECE
SHANKS OR
(BITS)

NECK

FINGER
HOOK

1st VALVE
2nd VALVE
3rd VALVE

TUNING
SLIDE

WATER
KEY

4. This is a professional's "trick of the trade" developed to add years of life to his instrument. Do not attempt unless you thoroughly understand the procedures and the ramifications!

A. Cleaning the Valves

If an instrument is old the valves are usually quite corroded and tarnished. This is not only destructive to the valves but also detrimental to the playing condition of the instrument. The valves can be cleaned by immersing them in a jar of pure vinegar and leaving them from one to eight hours, depending on the amount of corrosion which must be removed. When they are taken out they must be flushed thoroughly with clear water to remove all traces of vinegar.

B. Oiling the Valves

Oil to a valve in an instrument is as important as oil to a valve in an engine. The oil reduces friction and wear and retards corrosion. Some musicians use water or saliva. This is extremely dangerous because of the alkalies in water and the acids in saliva.

With a new instrument a very light oil should be used such as trombone slide oil. Even this at times is too thick and may be thinned with kerosene. As the instrument grows older, the oil should be thickened. This can be done by adding a few drops of key oil which can be purchased at any music store.

II. VALVE CAPS

The stuck valve cap is the result of the action of saliva on the metal, causing it to corrode and weld itself to the casing. If the cap is impossible to remove by hand, a rawhide mallet should be used to tap around the rim of the cap gently and directly on the top to loosen the corrosion. If this fails, penetrating oil should be added and the instrument allowed to stand overnight. The same process of tapping can then be repeated.

If both of these procedures fail the following steps can be taken.

Materials needed:
1. Pair of ordinary pliers
2. Piece of leather belt
3. Rawhide mallet
4. Petroleum jelly

Procedure:
1. Leave all valves and slides in the instrument, but remove the valve caps from as many valves as possible to give you room to work on the stuck cap.
2. Place the piece of leather belt around the rim of the stuck cap.
3. Grasp this with the pliers making sure the leather is between the pliers and the cap so as not to score the metal.
4. Twist to unscrew.

Figure 2.3

5. Clean the inside of the cap, including the threads on the valve casing, coat with petroleum jelly, and replace.

If all the caps are off at once, they should be kept in order because many times the caps will not be interchangeable.

III. WATER KEY SPRINGS

If the cork in a water key is seating correctly but still leaks, the tension of the water key spring should be checked.

Materials needed:
1. Needle nose pliers or roundnose pliers

Procedure:
1. Grasp the spring that extends outward behind the water key brace.
2. With the spring held tightly in the pliers, pull and bend the spring back and down.

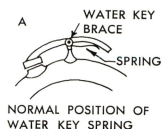

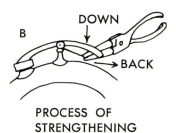

Figure 2.4

This will tighten the spring very nicely, but if it is still loose, the spring should be checked more thoroughly to see if it has a break in it. If broken, it had better be taken to a repairman who can replace the spring quite easily.

Rubber bands should never be used to hold the water key shut except in an extreme emergency. Rubber contains sulphur which will not only tarnish the entire instrument, but also will eat into the metal. This is also true of any rubber article left in a case, such as a pencil eraser or rubber bands.

IV. THE VALVES

A. Placement of the Key Guides

If the instrument completely fails to blow, the trouble can be traced to the valves which have been removed and replaced incorrectly. Removing the valves and then matching the valve numberings (see Plate IV) with the numbers on the valve casing will correct this. If the casings are not inscribed with numbers, it should be remembered that number one valve is the one nearest the mouthpiece.

Before replacing the valve the position of the "key guide" also should be checked. If the instrument has a single key guide (Plate IV) and a single slot inside the casing, there is no problem. There are several other spring-barrel types which can be replaced incorrectly, however, especially if the instrument is old.

One variation uses a key guide shaped like the letter "T" (Plate V). One side is larger than the other and must go into the casing accordingly. The correct placement of the valve in the casing can be assured by sighting into the empty casing to see which side has the large slot and which side the smaller. The other variation uses a three-pronged key guide (Plate V) using the same principle that one prong is larger than the others and so must be placed in its correct slot.

If the instrument is old and the key guides worn, the valves with the latter two variations can easily be replaced incorrectly.

B. Valve Damage

If a valve becomes stuck or "catches" as it moves up and down in the casing, the valve and its casing should first be checked to see that they are clean and well oiled. The most common cause of sticky valves is improper cleaning habits which allow a layer of corrosion and/or lime deposits to collect on the valve or its casing. If the trouble continues after cleaning, some damage has been done to the valve or its casing and should receive the attention of a skilled repairman. Even though the "catch" is small, no attempt to play the horn should be made. Continued use will wear off the plating on the valve and/or damage the casing and valve. A special check should be made to see if the problem is in the valve stem, which does at times become bent and binds against the valve cap as it is depressed. If this is the case, note the direction of the bend and, using a rawhide mallet, tap the valve stem back into place.

C. Valve Buttons

If an instrument produces a "click" as a valve is depressed, it is missing the felt and cork located in the valve button.[1] The felt washer and cork are there for two reasons—to regulate the depth of the stroke

---

1. If the click is present as the valve is released, it is usually caused by a loose valve cap. Tightening the cap will eliminate the noise.

PLATE IV — SINGLE KEYGUIDE VALVE

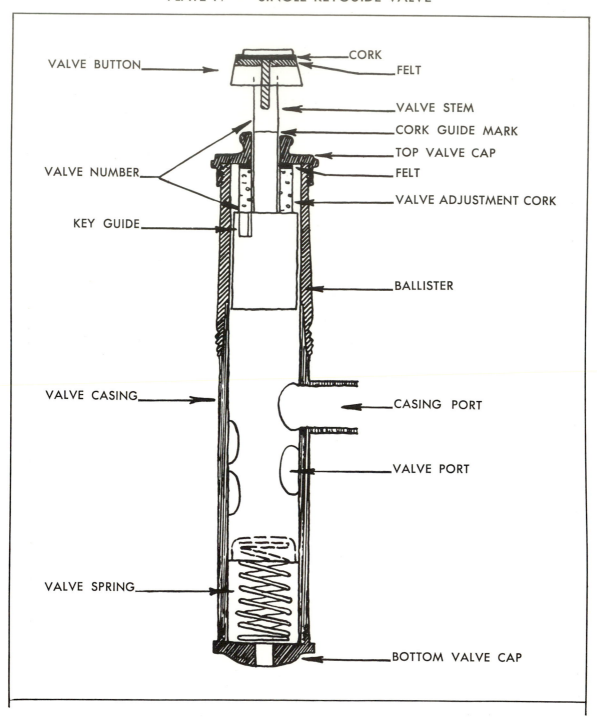

VALVE BUTTON

CORK

FELT

VALVE STEM

CORK GUIDE MARK

TOP VALVE CAP

FELT

VALVE NUMBER

VALVE ADJUSTMENT CORK

KEY GUIDE

BALLISTER

VALVE CASING

CASING PORT

VALVE PORT

VALVE SPRING

BOTTOM VALVE CAP

PLATE V—CONN CLICKLESS VALVE*

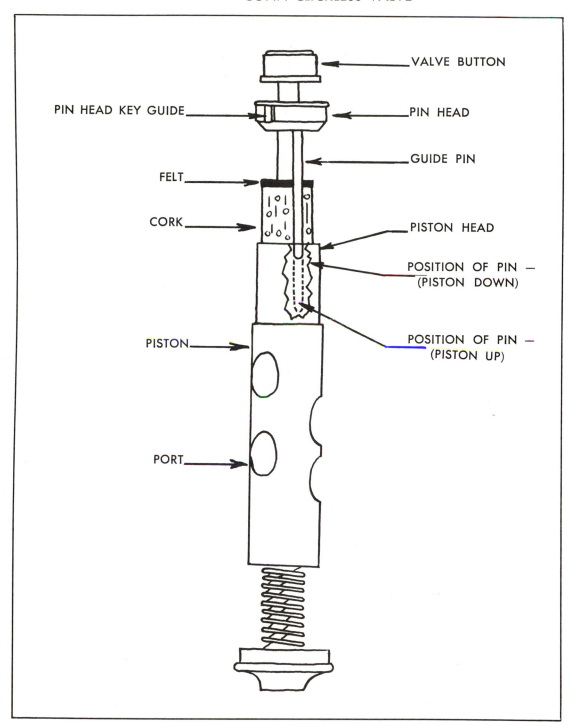

*Conn Corporation, *How to Care for Your Instrument* (C. G. Conn Ltd., 1942), Figure 6, p. 5.

PLATE VI—SPRING-BARREL TYPE VALVE
("Three Pronged" and "T" style)

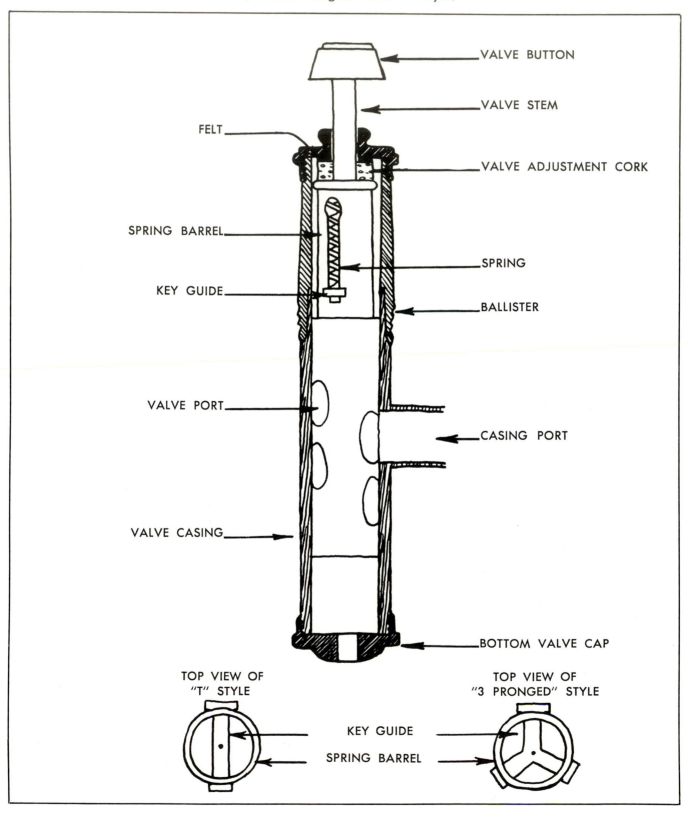

VALVE BUTTON

VALVE STEM

FELT

VALVE ADJUSTMENT CORK

SPRING BARREL

SPRING

KEY GUIDE

BALLISTER

VALVE PORT

CASING PORT

VALVE CASING

BOTTOM VALVE CAP

TOP VIEW OF "T" STYLE

TOP VIEW OF "3 PRONGED" STYLE

KEY GUIDE

SPRING BARREL

and to eliminate noise. Almost all instruments use this type of bumper except the Olds and some Conn instruments which place the cork and felt on the top valve cap. Other instrument manufacturers such as Besson and Holton, however, are using this type to give the illusion of a short action valve.

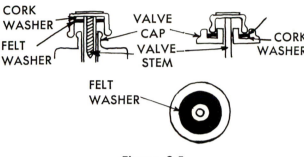

Figure 2.5

It is an excellent idea to keep an assortment of felts on hand for emergency replacements. As for the corks, the type that is on the top valve cap (Fig. 2.5, bottom) must be purchased precut from a repair shop. Cork for the standard type can be bought in tubes and then cut to size. The cork that goes into the valve button is cut to a 1/16″ thickness.

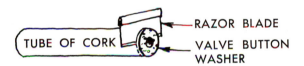

Figure 2.6

As Figure 2.7 shows, the cork lies underneath the felt. In replacing these items, the felt and cork shim should first be placed over the top of the valve stem. After the button is screwed on, the valve is depressed. This will force the cork shim and felt up into the button. If the felt and cork shim are put into the button rather than over the stem, they may wedge in between the top of the stem and the button thus making the depth of the stroke of the valve incorrect.

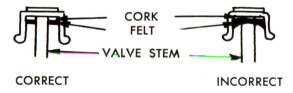

Figure 2.7

To further assure the correct thickness of the valve button cork, the second valve slide (see Plates I, II, and III) may be removed. By then depressing the second valve and sighting into the open ports, a check can be made. The ports in the valve should align perfectly with the ports of the casing.

D. Valve Adjustment Corks and Felts

Corks and felts are used also on the valve proper for the same reason as in the buttons—to regulate the stroke and to eliminate noise. To replace these the procedure is outlined following.

Materials needed:
1. Tube of cork
2. Razor blade
3. Valve felts

Procedure 1:

General: On each instrument the valve adjustment corks are exactly alike in thickness. Do not, however, trust them to be alike for a different instrument even though it is of the same type and make.

1. Take out one of the remaining valves, unscrew the valve button, take off the top valve cap, and remove the valve adjustment cork (see Plates IV, V, and VI).
2. Take a tube of valve cork and cut the proper length, using the one just removed as a pattern.

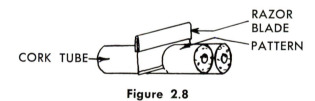

Figure 2.8

3. Fit the new cork over the valve stem and onto the valve (note position of corks in Plates IV, V, and VI).
4. On top of this place a valve felt.
5. Replace the top valve cap and screw on the valve button.
6. Replace the valve in its casing, screw down the valve cap, and sight across the top of the three valves to see if they are all the same height. To raise or lower the valve, add to or subtract from the adjustment cork.

CORRECT   INCORRECT

Figure 2.9

If the situation arises where there are no valve adjustment corks in any of the valves to use as patterns, or, because of poor tone quality, one is in doubt about the thickness or length of the corks that are on the valves, check for the proper thickness in the following way:

On some horns there is a cork guide marking cut around the valve stem (Plate IV). This mark should come flush with the rim of the top valve cap. If it is above, add a cork shim or cut a new and thicker one. If it is below the top valve cap, cut some off the adjustment cork.

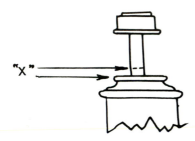

"X"

ADD "X" THICKNESS OF CORK ON TOP OF THE VALVE ADJUSTMENT CORK.

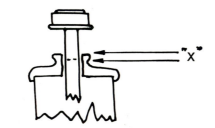

"X"

CUT OFF "X" THICKNESS FROM THE VALVE ADJUSTMENT CORK.

Figure 2.10

Procedure 2:

1. Take a piece of wire about six inches long and bend the last 1/2" at a right angle.

Figure 2.11

2. Place this in the empty casing of the second valve and insert the bent end into the lowest port that connects the second valve to the third valve.
3. Pull the wire up until the bent end catches on the top of the port.
4. With your thumb, mark on the wire where it comes flush with the top of the casing.

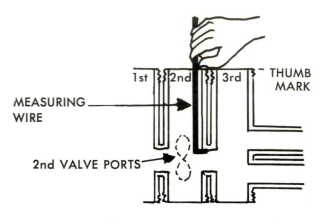

1st   2nd   3rd   THUMB MARK

MEASURING WIRE

2nd VALVE PORTS

Figure 2.12

5. Next take the corresponding valve (number two), check to see which port of the valve lines up with the port used for measuring in the casing, and insert the bent end of the wire into the valve port. Your thumb mark will be the height of the cork plus the felt.

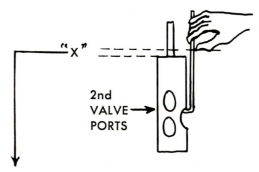

"X"

2nd VALVE PORTS

"X" EQUALS THE THICKNESS OF THE CORK PLUS THE FELT

Figure 2.13

6. "X" equals the thickness of the cork plus the felt.

With a Conn clickless valve (Plate VI) all procedures to replace an adjustment cork are the same except a groove must be cut down the length of the tube to permit the guide pin to move up and down. This can be done either by cutting a "V" down the length or by using a small needle file to file a groove into the side of the length of the cork.

CONN "CLICKLESS"
ADJUSTMENT CORK

Figure 2.14

E. Valve Springs

Many band directors are plagued with students who have taken their valves out to oil them and then have lost a valve spring or two.

It would be impractical for the band master or amateur repairman to keep a complete supply of springs on hand, for there are as many types of valve springs as there are makes of cornets, baritones, and basses. There is, however, one type which can be kept on hand and this is the type which fits in the bottom of the valve (Plate IV). Your local repairman or music store can supply you with a set of them (three) which can be kept on hand for emergencies.

The spring can be replaced in the casing either by removing the valve and dropping the spring in or by removing the bottom valve cap and pushing it in the bottom.

After the spring is in, the valve should be worked up and down to compare the tension with the other two valves. If the tension is different, the spring must be either weakened or strengthened.

Materials needed:
1. Wire cutters (pliers)
2. Petroleum jelly

Procedure: (To weaken the spring)
Remove the spring and, using the wire cutters, snip off one or two rings from the top. If more is needed to weaken the spring cut the same off the bottom.

CAUTION: Do not leave the spring so that the bearing surface is slanted. This will throw the valve at an uneven angle in the casing and cause extreme wear on one side. Take a pair of roundnose or ordinary pliers and bend the slanting section of wire down so it is level.

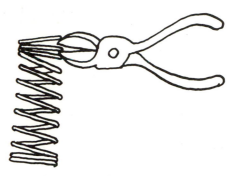

Figure 2.15

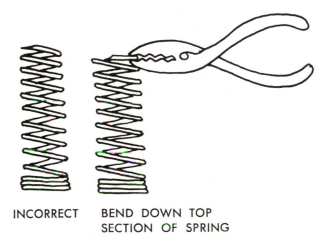

INCORRECT   BEND DOWN TOP
              SECTION OF SPRING

Figure 2.16

Procedure: (To strengthen the spring)
Grasp the spring at each end and stretch it to about twice its length (Step 1). Then compress it back together again (Step 2).

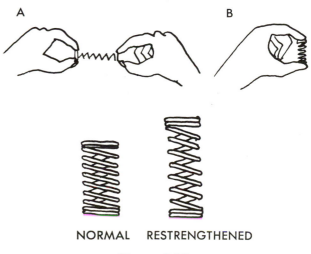

A   B

NORMAL   RESTRENGTHENED

Figure 2.17

Before replacing the spring, a *small* dab of petroleum jelly should be rubbed on the coiled ends of the spring to eliminate spring noise in the casing.

V. SPECIAL TIPS

1. A common problem with the Sousaphone is the stuck mouthpiece and bits. Should this occur, the mouthpiece and/or stuck bits can be placed on a soft block of wood and tapped with a rawhide mallet to loosen and separate them.
2. If a bag is used to carry the mouthpiece and bits of a bass horn, an effort should be made to keep them separate. A wool sock works well—one for the mouthpiece and one for the bits.
3. When removing or revolving the bell of a Sousaphone, be certain that all bell screws are loosened. When securing the bass bell in position, do not "overtighten" the bell screws. This will place undue pressure on the screw receptacles, which are soft soldered to the bell receiver, and cause them to break loose.
4. Never lay a valve instrument down so that it rests on an exposed valve slide; that is, the second valve of a cornet or trumpet.

VI. INSTRUMENT INSPECTION CHECK SHEET

Piston Valve Instruments

Instrument. . . . .   Serial Number. . . . .   Make. . . . .

School. . . . .   Private. . . . .   School or Manufacturer's Number . . . .

Finish. . . . .   Other Notations . . . .

	Needs
O.K.	Attention

MOUTHPIECE

1. Are the bore and cup clean?
2. Is the shank ovaled, bent, or dented?
3. Does it need plating?
4. Is the rim nicked or cut?
5. (Other comments)

SLIDES

1. Do all the slides work freely?
2. Are all the slides properly greased?
3. Are all water key corks in good condition?
4. Are all water key springs properly tensioned to close the key tightly?
5. Are there any large dents in the tubing?
6.

VALVES

1. Do all valves work freely?
2. Do any of the valves "click" when depressed or released?
3. Do the tops of all three valves align with one another?
4. Can the valve caps, top or bottom, be easily unscrewed?
5. Does the valve show signs of wearing in any particular spot?
6. Is the plating "flaking" off in spots on the valve?
7. Is the spring tension even on all valves?
8. Are all valves in their respective casings?
9.

GENERAL CONDITION

1. Are there any large dents in bell or bellcrook?
2. Are there any braces loose (unsoldered) or broken?
3. Is the lyre screw or finger hook screw missing?
4. Does the instrument need a thorough cleaning?
5. Are there any pitted holes in the mouthpipe?
6.

CASE

1. Does the case need repair (hinges, locks, and handle)?
2. Does the instrument fit securely in the case?
3. Are there any accessories lying loose in the case which can damage the instrument?
4.

OTHER COMMENTS

Date . . . .

(signature)

VII. CLASS PROJECT SHEET

Piston Valve Instruments

A. Know the names of the various parts of the instrument.

B. Be able to perform the following operations using the correct procedures, techniques, and tools.

1. Remove a stuck mouthpiece by:

   a. tapping with a rawhide mallet
   b. using pliers and a leather strap
   c. using a mouthpiece puller

2. Straighten a bent shank of a mouthpiece
3. Remove a stuck slide, clean, regrease, and replace
4. Replace a water key cork
5. Tighten a water key spring
6. Replace the cork and felt in a valve button
7. Replace the adjustment cork and felt on a valve using the old cork as a pattern
8. Replace the adjustment cork and felt on a valve without using the old cork as a pattern
9. Strengthen and weaken a valve spring
10. Remove a stuck valve cap

C. Demonstrate the correct methods and procedures for the following operations.

1. Assemble and disassemble the mouthpiece and the instrument
2. Oil the valves
3. Grease the slides
4. Clean the instrument inside and out with the correct attention given to a silver or lacquered finish

D. General.

Be able to give instruction on the daily care and maintenance of the piston valve instrument with emphasis on eliminating the common errors or bad habits which lead to the need for repair work.

Chapter 3

TROMBONE

PLATE VII—TROMBONE

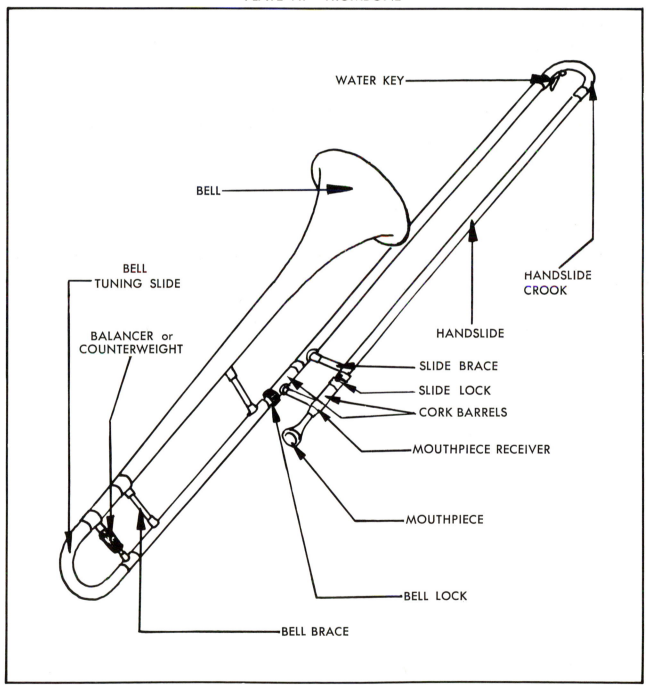

WATER KEY

BELL

BELL
TUNING SLIDE

BALANCER or
COUNTERWEIGHT

HANDSLIDE
CROOK

HANDSLIDE

SLIDE BRACE

SLIDE LOCK

CORK BARRELS

MOUTHPIECE RECEIVER

MOUTHPIECE

BELL LOCK

BELL BRACE

I. CLEANING AND LUBRICATION

The neglect in properly cleaning the instrument, next to a bent slide, is a major cause for many unnecessary repair bills.

The heart of the trombone is the handslide. These slides are manufactured and assembled with great care and precision. The body of the slide consists of four brass tubes about three feet in length. The outside slide is approximately .011″ (eleven thousandths of an inch) thick (on lightweight instruments it is about half of this) and the inside slide is about .008″ thick. These two tubes must be placed one inside the other and be able to move freely back and forth with clearance on each side of .003″, or about the thickness of one human hair. With this in mind, it is quite natural that in the cleaning process special attention must be given the handslides; however, it is necessary to inspect all other parts and sections of the instrument to see that they are not badly worn or working improperly. If repairs are imminent, refer to the following respective topics in the chapter.

The process for cleaning a trombone is as follows.

Materials needed:

1. Trombone cleaning rod
2. Slide oil
3. Petroleum jelly
4. Several soft pieces of cloth about three feet long and about seven inches wide
5. Trombone flexible brush
6. Castile soap

Procedure: (Disassembling and cleaning)

1. Have a large basin or sink of lukewarm, sudsy water.

   CAUTION: Do not use hot water. This will cause the lacquer on a brass instrument to peel. Even some silver instruments have lacquer on them, specifically on the bell. Many strong laundry soaps will have the same effect. It is best to use a castile soap or a mild detergent.

2. Remove the bell tuning slide from the bell section and submerge both the bell section and the tuning slide in the water. Then use the flexible brush to flush out any foreign matter inside the tubing. After this rinse in clear water to remove the soap and remaining grime and wipe both parts dry.

3. Take one of the pieces of cloth and thread and wind it onto the trombone cleaning rod.

Be sure the entire rod, particularly the tip, is well covered.

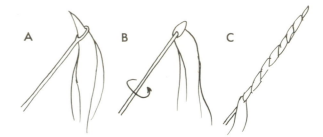

Figure 3.1

4. Take the handslides, release the slide lock, and separate the two slides.
5. Working with the outside slide first, fill the slide with soapy water and run the flexible brush back and forth through the slide crook to loosen foreign matter. Then dump out the soapy water and run clean water through the slide until it comes out clear. Repeat this procedure several times (see special cleaning of handslide crook).
6. Next take the cleaning rod, wound with the cloth, and insert it into one of the tubes. Be sure you are gripping the tube close to the open end. Be sure also that the hand that is holding the rod is holding the cloth. The cloth and rod must move in and out together.

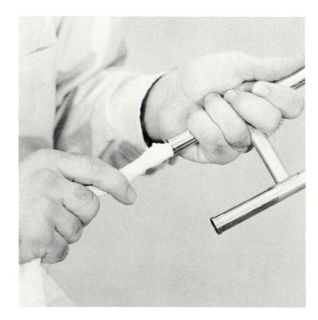

Figure 3.2

7. Push the rod in and out with a twisting motion. Change the cloth before it becomes extremely soiled. Repeat the process until the cloth remains clean. When one side is clean, repeat the process in the other tube.

8. Place the outside handslide on a clean cloth and take the inside slide. In the same manner as above, clean the inside of these tubes. (This is an area seldom cleaned by most trombonists and it is the reason for much slide trouble because foreign matter in this area is blown directly into the small clearance between the inside and outside slide. This also is the area in which most of the saliva collects as the saliva that goes by this area is blown out of the crook through the water key.) A smaller width of cloth should be used here—keep in mind *never* to force the rod into the tube. If the cleaning rod is too large, a long flexible brush may be used.

9. Clean out the cork barrels and the bumper corks by using a pipe cleaner dipped in oil or a piece of Scotch tape fastened to a thin stick.

10. The last step is to take one more clean cloth and wipe off the inside slides.

A. Special Cleaning of Handslide Crook

A technique that will do an even better job of cleaning the crook of the handslide than the flexible brush is the use of a wet paper slug, water, and the hydraulic pump principle.

Procedure:

1. Soak and wad up a piece of paper (toweling or newspaper) that is just large enough to fit snugly into one of the outer slide tubings.

2. Using the inner slide, ram this into the tubing as far as it will go.

3. Fill this same tubing with water.

4. Insert only one of the tubes of the inner slide about two inches into the water filled tube of the outer handslide.

5. Hold the thumb over the end of the inner slide tube and quickly ram the two slides together. The pressure of air and water against the paper slug will send it around the crook and out the other tubing. Needless to say, this should be done in an area where water can be spilled. Also, be certain that the open tub-

ing of the outer handslide is pointed away from the body. If the paper slug fails to come out of the opposite tube, into which it was placed, repeat the "pump" action.

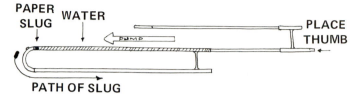

Figure 3.3

Procedure: (Greasing, oiling, and assembling)

1. After you have wiped the inside slide clean, apply three or four drops of good slide oil on one of the "stockings" of the slide.[1]

Figure 3.4

Some musicians prefer to use cold cream and water instead of oil. This works well for professional musicians, but is not recommended for students; too much cold cream will gum up the slide. The instrument also must be cleaned more often because some cold creams become sticky after a short time. The dangers of using water in an instrument have been discussed in the previous chapter.

2. Insert the inside slide into the proper outside slide and work it in and out as well as around. The oil on the slide may pick up some dust or grime that has been missed by the cleaning rod; therefore, listen carefully for any slide noises (grating). If such noise occurs, separate the slides, wipe the inside slides clean, run the rod through the outside slides, oil again, and replace.

Repeat this procedure with the other slide. When both slides work freely and easily, independently, put them together and lock them.

---

1. Note that you do not oil the entire slide area, only the "sock."

NOTE: On some trombones it is impossible to reverse the inside slides in the outside slides because one side is larger than the other. On many trombones, however, the handslides are the same and thus interchangeable. To avoid getting the slides reversed, match the longest tube of the inside slide with the outside slide which has the water key on it.

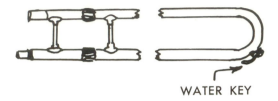

WATER KEY

Figure 3.5

3. Next take the bell section and the bell tuning slide. Smear a small dab of petroleum jelly on the bearing surface of the tuning slide and insert one side only into its proper tubing. Work this in and out until all heavy friction is gone. Repeat this with the other side of the slide. When both sides work freely, replace the bell tuning slide as previously instructed.

4. The last step is to connect the bell section to the handslides. In so doing do not jam the handslide tenon into the slide receiver (see Plate VII). Constant abuse of this sort will eventually flange the receiver tube and soon a leak will develop as well as a loose fit. Instead, insert the tenon into the receiver and rotate the slides back and forth as you push the two parts together. If the trombone has a bell lock, it will force them together without twisting.

B. Bumper Corks

These are located in the cork barrel and serve two purposes: they eliminate shock and noise as the trombone is pulled into the first position and, to some degree, bring the first position tones in tune.

Often a trombone will develop an unexplainable drag which disappears after the slide is wiped clean only to return again later. This can be traced to either dirt in the handslide crook which has been blown into the slide section (the remedy for this was discussed under Cleaning), or dirt or grinding powder used by the manufacturer which has collected on the bumper corks and been dragged down into the slide area by the action of the slide.

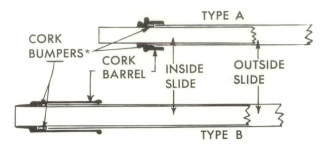

*Some trombone slides of this type employ a spring instead of a cork.

Figure 3.6

The bumper corks and the cork barrel should be cleaned frequently. This can be done by using a pipe cleaner dipped in oil. Better still is a piece of Scotch tape fastened to a matchstick, or something similar, with the sticky side out. This will pick up any loose dirt, grime, or dust when worked around inside the barrel.

C. Bumper Cork Replacement

If the handslide produces a sharp click as it is snapped into first position, one or more bumper corks is either worn or missing and should be replaced. In addition, if the instrument is old and there is suspicion that the corks are extremely impregnated with oil, dust, or other foreign matter, new corks should be installed.

Materials needed:
1. Sheet of cork 3/32″ thick
2. Razor blade
3. Bumper cork removing tool

BUMPER CORK REMOVING TOOL

Figure 3.7

Procedure:
1. Remove the inner from the outer slide. If possible, unscrew and remove the slide lock.
2. Insert the tool, point first, over one of the inside slides and slide it up into the cork barrel.
3. Rotate the tool until it grabs or bites into the bumper cork. Continue rotating the tool as it is withdrawn.

4. This most likely will have to be done several times to remove the entire cork. Be certain the barrel is absolutely clean and clear before proceeding.

5. Repeat this process on the other slide. *Never replace only one bumper cork.*

6. Using an old piece of cork that has been removed, cut two strips of new cork equal to the width of the old one. Cut the strips so that the grain runs parallel to the cut.

← GRAIN →

Figure 3.8

7. With the rawhide mallet, pound the cork strip to soften and break up the brittle fibers in it.

8. Wrap the cork strip around the inside slide close to the cork barrel and trim the excess amount so that both ends meet evenly with no gap or overlap.

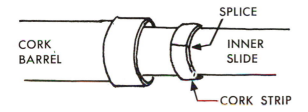

Figure 3.9

9. Place the outer slide over the respective inner slide and ram the cork down and into the cork barrel.

NOTE:

1. If the slide cannot be locked, the cork is too wide. Remove and use a narrower piece.
2. If the slide, when locked, has a small amount of play in it, the cork is too narrow. Remove and use a wider piece.

When properly installed the slides, when locked, should be tight without any play.

II. HANDSLIDE TROUBLE

Cleaning the bumper corks and the cork barrel will solve some of the troubles that occur with a trombone slide. There are, however, many other reasons why a slide may not work properly. A bad habit that also should be watched for is the practice of the trombonist forcefully setting his horn down slide first on the floor, after playing or while resting between measures or tunes. This springs the slides outward and will cause a severe "drag" in the slide action, especially in the sixth and seventh positions.

A correct diagnosis of the trouble by a competent repairman can eliminate the cause completely and avert serious damage. Any handslide problems that cannot be remedied by cleaning should be taken to a repairman immediately.

When buying a used trombone it is quite natural to check the condition of the handslide. In this process should come the consideration of the amount of wear to the inner slides. Two tests will give a reasonable assurance that a slide is functioning properly without air being wasted due to wear on the metal plating of the stockings.

Procedure 1:

Hold the heel of the hand and thumb over both ends of the assembled handslide. Then throw the outer slide out. If there is close tolerance between the two slides, the outer one will bounce back, if not the outer slide will remain out or will show little return—thus indicating wear on the stockings and air seepage.

Procedure 2:

Set the assembled handslides on the floor and pull the inner slides about half the way up and out. Close off one of the tubes of the inner slide with the hand; with the mouth, suck in on the outer tubing. If the slide is in good condition, the suction created should raise the outer slide up and off the floor.

III. SPECIAL TIPS

The appearance of water spots on the bell of an instrument is a visual sign that the trombonist is not draining the slide before it is placed in the case. This neglect can cause a multitude of problems such as corrosion to the inner slides and the inner part of the outside slides, deterioration of the water key cork, and damage to the lining and case itself.

IV. INSTRUMENT INSPECTION CHECK SHEET

Trombone

Instrument. . . . .   Serial Number. . . . .   Make. . . . .

School. . . . .   Private. . . . .   School or Manufacturer's Number . . . .

Finish. . . . .   Other Notations   . . . .

| | Needs | MOUTHPIECE |
| O.K. | Attention | |

MOUTHPIECE

. . . . .1. Are the bore and cup clean?
. . . . .2. Is the shank ovaled, bent, or dented?
. . . . .3. Does it need plating?
. . . . .4. Is the rim nicked or cut?
. . . . .5. (Other comments)

TUNING SLIDES

. . . . .1. Does the slide (or slides) work freely?
. . . . .2. Is the slide (or slides) properly greased?
. . . . .3. Are there any large dents in the tubing?
. . . . .4.

HANDSLIDE

. . . . .1. Does the slide work freely in all positions without "dragging" or "grating"?
. . . . .2. Does the slide "click" when pulled up fast into first position?
. . . . .3. Is the water key cork in good condition?
. . . . .4. Is the water key spring properly tensioned to close the key tightly?
. . . . .5. Does the slide lock hold the slides together securely?
. . . . .6. Is the plating on the inside slides "flaking" off?
. . . . .7. Is the bore of the tubing on the inside slides dirty?
. . . . .8.

GENERAL CONDITION

. . . . .1. Are there any dents in the bell or tubing?
. . . . .2. Are there any braces loose (unsoldered) or broken?
. . . . .3. Does the instrument need a thorough cleaning?
. . . . .4.

CASE

. . . . .1. Does the case need repair (hinges, locks, and handle)?
. . . . .2. Does the instrument fit securely in the case?
. . . . .3. Are there any accessories lying loose in the case which can dent the instrument?
. . . . .4.

OTHER COMMENTS

Date . . . .
                                                                                          (signature)

V. CLASS PROJECT SHEET

Trombone

A. Know the names of the various parts of the instrument.

B. Be able to perform the following operation using the correct procedures, techniques, and tools.

   1. Remove a stuck mouthpiece by:

      a. tapping with a rawhide mallet
      b. using pliers and a leather strap
      c. using a mouthpiece puller

   2. Straighten a bent shank of a mouthpiece
   3. Remove a stuck tuning slide, clean, regrease, and replace
   4. Replace a water key cork
   5. Replace the bumper corks

C. Demonstrate the correct methods and procedures for the following operations.

   1. Assemble and disassemble the instrument
   2. Oil the handslides
   3. Remove, grease and replace the tuning slide
   4. Clean the instrument inside and out with the correct attention given to a silver or lacquered finish

D. General.

Be able to give instructions on the daily care and maintenance of the trombone with emphasis on eliminating the common errors or bad habits which lead to the need for repair work.

Chapter 4

FRENCH HORN

PLATE VIII—FRENCH HORN

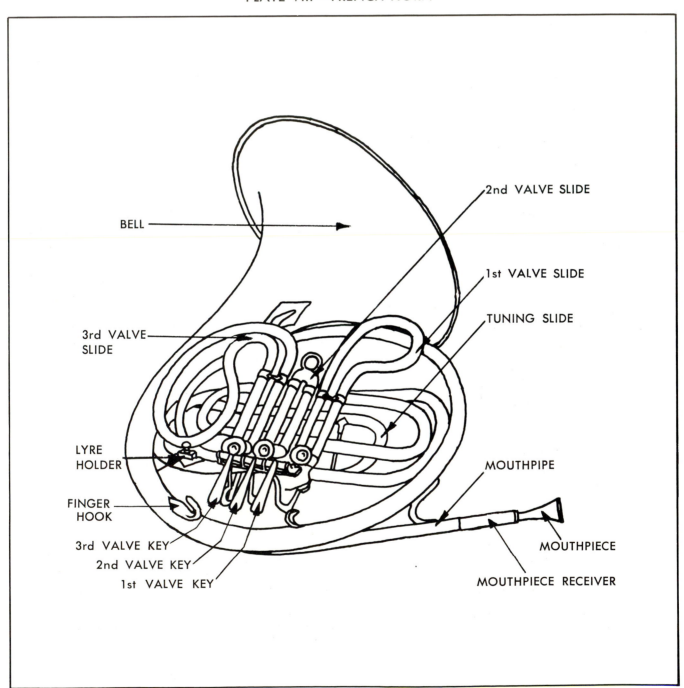

BELL

2nd VALVE SLIDE

1st VALVE SLIDE

TUNING SLIDE

3rd VALVE SLIDE

LYRE HOLDER

FINGER HOOK

3rd VALVE KEY

2nd VALVE KEY

1st VALVE KEY

MOUTHPIPE

MOUTHPIECE

MOUTHPIECE RECEIVER

I. CLEANING AND LUBRICATION

The lack of water keys on the French horn has made the collection of moisture a real problem to contend with. The valves, which are not as accessible as those on piston valve instruments, receive little if any cleaning or lubricating attention. The broken valve string, which is a very common repair problem, is often caused because a valve has become stuck and the attempts to free it have been done by forcibly depressing the valve key.

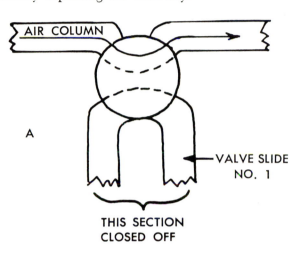

VALVE KEY IN NORMAL POSITION

Figure 4.1

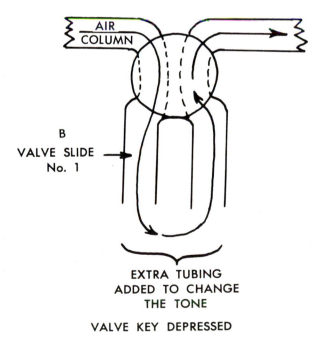

EXTRA TUBING
ADDED TO CHANGE
THE TONE

VALVE KEY DEPRESSED

Figure 4.2

A. The Valves

Instead of a piston-type valve, as used in other brass instruments, the French horn employs a type of valve which rotates to change the stream of air. As with other valve instruments, this is the heart of the horn, and should be given special and frequent care.

1. Oiling the Valves—Temporary

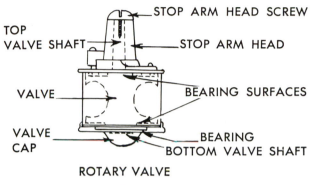

ROTARY VALVE

Figure 4.3

The bearing surface on both ends of the valve should be oiled every few weeks. This can be done on the bottom side by removing the bottom valve cap and applying oil to the exposed shaft (see Fig. 4.4).[1]

As the oil is applied, the valve should be rotated so the oil can work down inside and around the shaft. To oil the top bearing, the stop arm head screw is loosened about three turns; the stop arm head is then lifted enough so that the oil can run in on top of the bearing surface.

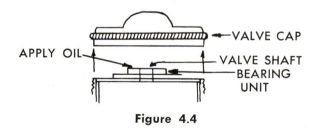

Figure 4.4

2. Oiling the Valves—Thorough

This process of removing, cleaning, and oiling the valves on the French horn is a complicated one and must be followed carefully step-by-step.

---

1. Use "key oil" rather than valve oil—it will last longer and work more effectively.

Materials needed:

1. Rawhide mallet
2. Two screwdrivers (one narrow-blade, one wide-blade)
3. Key oil
4. Petroleum jelly
5. Clean rags
6. Penetrating oil
7. Pint jar of vinegar

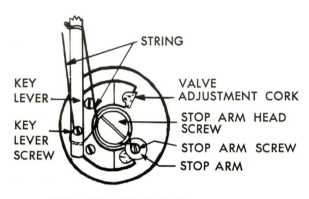

TOP VIEW OF VALVE

Figure 4.5

Procedure: (Disassembling)

1. Loosen both the key lever screw and the stop arm screw and pull the string loose. After the string is removed, tighten the screws so they will not be lost in the operation.
2. Grasp the stop arm between the fingers to prevent squashing the valve adjusting corks and, using a thin-bladed screwdriver, loosen the stop arm head screw about four turns.
3. Next, turn the instrument over and unscrew the valve cap. If it is struck, refer to Section D of this chapter which pertains to stuck valve caps.
4. Turn the instrument over, take the rawhide mallet and tap firmly on the top of the stop arm head screw. This will push the valve down and force the bearing unit down and out. Be sure the hand is cupped underneath the valve to catch the bearing as it drops out.
5. After placing the bearing in a safe place, unscrew the head screw completely. This will allow the valve to drop out. If the valve sticks, screw the stop arm head screw back in about two turns, gently tap the head of the screw and the valve will be forced out. To remove

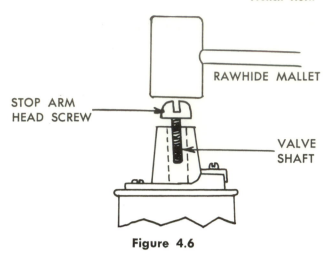

Figure 4.6

the valve completely, unscrew the stop arm head screw and pull the valve out.

Now, discounting the string, there should be five separate pieces: (1) the stop arm head screw, (2) the stop arm head, (3) the valve itself, (4) the bearing unit, and (5) the valve cap (see Fig. 4.7).

6. Inspect the valve, the bearing unit, and the valve cap for signs of corrosion. If some is present, submerge these three parts in vinegar and allow them to soak for about half an hour or so, depending on the amount of corrosion to be removed. If they appear to be free of corrosion simply wipe off the old grease and grime and set them aside.
7. Wipe out the inside of the valve casing with a clean cloth.

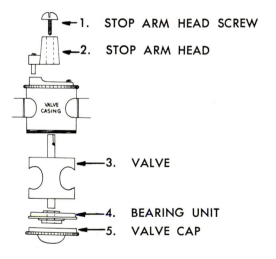

Figure 4.7

Procedure: (Greasing, oiling, and assembling)

1. Apply a liberal amount of petroleum jelly on the bearing ridges of the valve, then add two or three drops of key oil to this. The petroleum jelly alone is too gummy and the oil alone is too thin; together they make a very suitable and lasting lubricant.

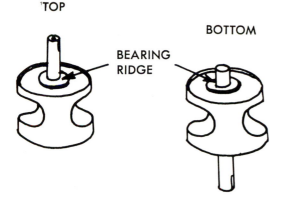

Figure 4.8

2. Apply a few drops of oil also to the sides of valve. This is not for friction purposes, because the valve does not come in real contact with the sides of the casing as do piston-type valves, but rather for the purpose of retarding corrosion and creating an airtight seal.

3. Slip the valve into the valve casing and twirl it back and forth to spread the lubricant. The valve should spin freely in the casing. If it does not, there still is some corrosion or foreign matter that must be cleaned out.

4. Next take the bearing unit, smear a minute amount of petroleum jelly around the inside of the hole, and add a few drops of oil on top of it.

Figure 4.9

5. In replacing the bearing unit, be sure to locate on the edge of the valve casing a small mark that must coincide with the mark made on the bearing unit itself. Some instruments have a small key on the bearing unit which fits into a slot in the casing.

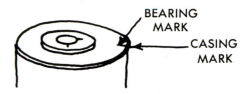

Figure 4.10

NOTE: The bearing unit, if not properly replaced, will bind and cause the valve to stick. If this happens, turn the horn over and tap on top of the valve stem to knock the bearing unit out. Then replace the unit, being careful to seat it properly and evenly. It can then be tapped into place with the rawhide mallet.

A large thread spool is an excellent tool for tapping the bearing unit into place. Make certain the hole in the spool is large enough to fit over the valve shaft. Lay the bearing into position, place the spool over the shaft, and tap.

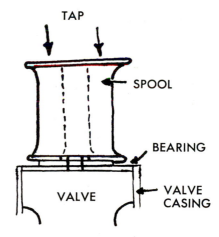

Figure 4.11

6. Once the bearing unit is on, spin the valve again to make sure it still is free. Then slip the stop arm head onto the valve stem. The head must be placed on so that the stop arm is between the two valve adjustment corks (see Fig. 4.5).

7. Rotate the valve back and forth to make sure again the valve still is operating freely before screwing in the stop arm head screw.

8. Turn the instrument over and, after smearing a little petroleum jelly on the inside threads, screw on the valve cap.

The last step is to restring the valve. Since a broken valve string is the most common problem with the French horn, it will be treated separately.

II. VALVE RESTRINGING

Materials needed:

1. Braided fishline (about 30-lb. test)
2. Knife
3. Screwdriver (small blade)

Procedure:

1. Loosen both the stop arm screw and the key lever screw and remove the broken string (see Fig. 4.5).
2. Cut a piece of fishline seven to eight inches long and tie a double knot in one end, large enough so that the string will not slip through the hole in the key lever. Feed the string through the hole with the knot on the opposite side from the valve.
3. After the string has been fed through the hole, give it a firm tug to set the knot in the hole and to make certain it does not pull through. Then run the string around behind the stop

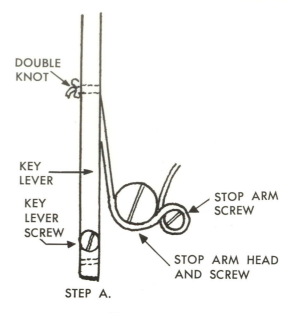

DOUBLE KNOT

KEY LEVER

KEY LEVER SCREW

STOP ARM SCREW

STOP ARM HEAD AND SCREW

STEP A.

Figure 4.13

arm head, twist a loop in the string and slip it over the top of the stop arm screw.

NOTE:

1. The direction of the string and the correct overlapping.
2. Do not tighten this screw at this time.
4. Next, continue circling the stop arm head with the string and feed it through the hole in the end of the key lever.

Figure 4.14

5. Loop the string around the key lever screw in a clockwise direction, pull it taut and tighten the screw. Leave about an inch and a half of string for adjusting purposes and cut off the rest.

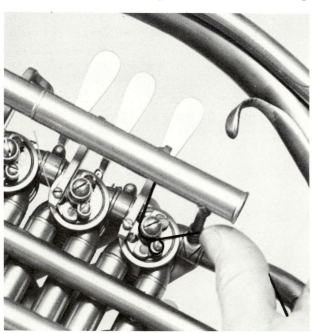

Figure 4.12

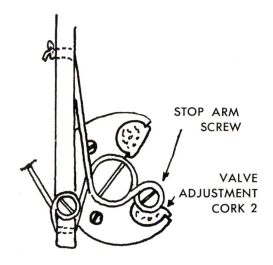

Figure 4.15

6. Check and adjust the height of the valve key. As the stop arm screw is held against the no. 2 valve adjustment cork, move the valve key to the proper height. Hold the key in this position and tighten the stop arm screw.

Should any or all valve keys need to be lowered or raised, simply loosen the stop arm screw, adjust the key, and retighten the screw.

NOTE: This procedure may be followed for the cleaning, oiling, and restringing of French horn thumb valves, bass trombone trigger valves, and tuba rotary valves.

III. VALVE ALIGNING

When a valve key is depressed on the French horn the valve rotates in the casing, changing the stream of air from one section of tubing to another (see Fig. 4.1). The stroke or distance the valve turns is governed by two adjustment corks on the outside of the valve (see Fig. 4.5). If either of these corks is lost or worn, the valve does not align properly with the tubings and the true intonation of the horn is distorted.

To determine whether the corks are of the proper thickness, the valve cap must be unscrewed and removed. It is then possible to check the position of the valve by two marks on the valve shaft. These marks are located on the raised ridge of the bearing unit at a 45-degree angle from one another.

When the valve key is up, one of the marks should be perfectly in line with the bearing unit mark. When

the valve key is depressed, the shaft will spin 90 degrees, and the other shaft mark should align with the bearing mark.

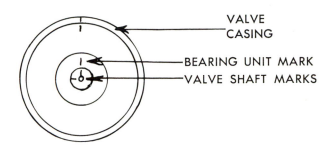

Figure 4.16

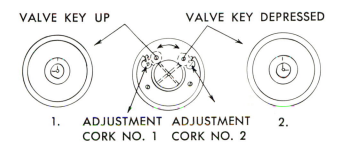

Figure 4.17

Considering diagram 1, Figure 4.17 first, if the valve shaft mark falls to the right of the bearing mark, cut off a small amount of adjustment cork 1 until the marks align. If the shaft mark falls to the left, the adjustment cork is too small and a new and larger cork must be installed. When the key is depressed (diagram 2) and the shaft mark stops short of the bearing mark or to the left, cut off a small amount of adjustment cork 2. If the shaft mark stops to the right of the bearing mark, the cork again is too small and must be replaced with a larger one.

A. Replacing Valve Adjustment Corks

Materials needed:
1. Stick of cork about 1/4" in diameter
2. Razor blade

Procedure:
1. Clean out the old cork and grime from the jaw area.
2. Wedge the end of the stick of cork upright into the jaw.
3. Slice off the excess cork flush with the top of the jaw.

TUBE OF CORK

Figure 4.18

4. Turn the horn over and check the adjustment marks as explained in the preceding section.

Tubes of neoprene rubber can also be used quite successfully instead of the cork tubing. There is a small amount of bounce, which is objectionable to some who have used it, but it will greatly outlast cork. The process of replacing the bumper with this material is the same.

IV. VALVE CAPS

The stuck valve cap is caused by the action of saliva on the metal, causing it to corrode and weld itself to the casing. If the cap is impossible to remove by hand, a rawhide mallet should be used to tap gently around the rim of the cap and directly on the top to loosen the corrosion. If this fails, penetrating oil should be added and the instrument allowed to stand overnight. The same process of tapping can then be repeated.

If both of these procedures fail, the following steps can be taken.

Materials needed:

1. Pair of ordinary pliers
2. Piece of leather belt
3. Rawhide mallet

Procedure:

1. Leave all valves and slides in the instrument, but remove the valve caps from as many valves as possible to give you room to work on the stuck cap.
2. Place the piece of leather belt around the rim of the stuck cap.
3. Grasp this with the pliers making sure the leather is between the pliers and the cap so as not to score the metal.
4. Twist to unscrew.

If all the caps are off at once, they should be kept in order because many times the caps will not be interchangeable.

V. THE BODY

The French horn has smaller tubing than the other brasses, thus even the smallest amount of foreign matter that collects in the tubing will impair the tone and intonation. The French horn also has more tubing and crooks, but no spit valves to drain saliva and moisture from the horn. It is readily seen what this does to the performance of the instrument. Most of the damage is caused by acids in the saliva. Much of this water can be removed by pulling the slides, but water that collects in the valve area deposits a coating of lime and corrosion on the valves. This, if allowed to remain too long, will retard the action of the valves and eventually cause them to "freeze."

Many times it is desirable to clean the valves and restring them without cleaning the entire instrument. The process of removing, cleaning, lubricating, replacing, and adjusting the valves has been outlined previously. The remainder of the instrument, the body and slides, are dealt with as follows.

Materials needed:

1. Flexible brush
2. Petroleum jelly
3. Several clean rags
4. Castile soap or mild detergent

Procedure:

1. Use a large basin filled with lukewarm, sudsy water.

CAUTION: Do not use hot water; this will cause the lacquer to peel on a brass instrument. Even some silver instruments have lacquer on them, specifically on the bell. Many strong laundry soaps will have the same effect. It is best, therefore, to use a castile soap or a mild detergent.

2. Pull all slides and wipe them free of old grease. If the instrument is a double horn, use some method to lay out the slides so as not to get them mixed up and, consequently, put back in the wrong tubing.
3. Submerge the body of the instrument in the warm water and allow it to soak for about ten minutes. While the horn is soaking, dip the slides in the water and run the flexible brush through them. Repeat this process until all foreign matter is removed from the inside of the slide tubing, then rinse with clear water.

4. After the slides are wiped dry and put aside, take the body of the horn and repeat the same process as with the slides—run the flexible brush through all the tubings and flush with clean, clear water.
5. Wipe the horn dry.
6. It is at this point that the valves should be replaced and restrung (see Sections I and II).
7. Before replacing the slides, coat the bearing surfaces with a thin coat of petroleum jelly and work in only one side at a time. When both tubes of the slide work freely independently, wipe them clean, regrease, and replace the slide.

VI. SPECIAL TIPS

1. We have discussed the procedure for cleaning the valves, but an ounce of prevention is worth a pound of cure. To prevent corrosion, each of the valve slides can be removed and, using an eye dropper, several drops of penetrating oil can be squirted down the slide tube onto the valve— a few drops with the valve key depressed, then a few with the key released. To be effective, this should be done every three or four weeks, depending upon use.
2. While the horn is in its case, it should be well blocked and strapped and all accessories should be in a separate compartment or wrapped in cloths. The bell of the French horn is especially thin and soft and thus easily dented. A dent in the bell, unless extremely large, is best left alone because it will not affect the playing qualities of the horn. If it is taken to a repair shop the dent is either rubbed or pounded out. This leaves a hard spot in the bell, and a number of such spots will affect the coloring and resonance of the instrument's tone.
3. A good trick used by some French horn players is to make a small plug that will fit securely into the end of the mouthpiece receiver when the instrument is put in the case. This plug prevents any leftover moisture from collecting and running out

into the case; it also prevents any dust or grime from collecting in the lip of the mouthpipe to be blown into the instrument when it is played later.
4. A protective covering often is used around the tubing in the area of the finger hook. This is the section of the horn subjected to perspiration acids from the hand. Several devices have been used, including plastic friction tape and even spiral plastic telephone cord covers. Any protection is well worth the effort. Care should be taken, however, that the material used is not rubber or a composition containing rubber. The sulphur in rubber will cause the metal to corrode quickly and, if left for some time, quite severely.
5. To prevent acids from forming on the inside of the mouthpipe, a few drops of oil can be placed in the mouthpipe. The instrument is then tilted and rotated so the oil will spread evenly in the tube as it flows through. This procedure is also recommended for breaking in a new instrument.
6. Some directors still use the French horn with an E♭ slide. Others leave the E♭ slide in the case where it is a temptation for a student to switch slides for the sake of curiosity. If there is any doubt as to which is the E♭ slide and which is the F, bear in mind that E♭ is lower in pitch than F and, therefore, requires more tubing. Size, then, is the quickest way to tell the difference.

   Another important factor to remember if the E♭ slide is used is that all of the valve slides must be pulled out a certain amount to bring the instrument into the correct key. Usually a small groove can be found around the shank of each slide to be used as a guide.
7. Should a rotary valve become frozen, do not attempt to force it free by depressing the valve key. Rather, loosen the stop arm head screw about a quarter of a turn and tap the top of it with a rawhide mallet. This will jar the valve loose. Oil should be applied then to both bearing areas. This problem should be a warning that the valves are in need of an immediate thorough cleaning and oiling.

VII. INSTRUMENT INSPECTION CHECK SHEET

French Horn

Instrument...................................... Serial Number..................... Make.............

School.......... Private.......... School or Manufacturer's Number ....

Finish............................... Other Notations ....

O.K.	Needs Attention		

MOUTHPIECE

........................1. Are the bore and cup clean?
........................2. Is the shank ovaled, bent, or dented?
........................3. Does it need plating?
........................4. Is the rim nicked or cut?
........................5. (Other comments)

SLIDES

........................1. Do all the slides work freely?
........................2. Are all the slides properly greased?
........................3. Are there any large dents in the tubing?
........................4. Are all slides in the correct places and order?
........................5.

VALVES

........................1. Do all valves rotate freely when keys are depressed?
........................2. Are all valves properly strung with no lost action?
........................3. Can the bottom valve caps be easily unscrewed?
........................4. Are there any missing or badly worn valve bumper (adjustment) corks?
........................5. Do all three of the valve keys lie at the same level?
........................6. Is the tension even on all valve keys?
........................7.

GENERAL CONDITION

........................1. Are there any large dents in the bell or tubing?
........................2. Are there any braces loose (unsoldered) or broken?
........................3. Is the lyre screw missing?
........................4. Does the instrument need a thorough cleaning?
........................5.

CASE

........................1. Does the case need repair (hinges, locks, and handle)?
........................2. Does the instrument fit securely in the case?
........................3. Are there any accessories lying loose in the case which can dent the instrument?
........................4.

OTHER COMMENTS

Date ....
                                                                (signature)

VIII. CLASS PROJECT SHEET

French Horn

A. Know the names of the various parts of the instrument.

B. Be able to perform the following operations using the correct procedures, techniques, and tools.

    1. Remove a stuck mouthpiece by:

        a. tapping with a rawhide mallet
        b. using pliers and a leather strap
        c. using a mouthpiece puller

    2. Straighten a bent shank of a mouthpiece
    3. Remove a stuck slide, clean, regrease, and replace
    4. Replace a pair of valve adjustment corks and correctly align the valve
    5. Completely disassemble, clean, lubricate, and reassemble a valve and its component parts
    6. Restring a valve and its key

C. Demonstrate and correct methods and procedures for the following operations.

    1. Assemble and disassemble the mouthpiece and the instrument
    2. Oil the valves
    3. Grease the slides
    4. Clean the instrument inside and out with the correct attention given to a silver or lacquered finish

D. General.
Be able to give instruction on the daily care and maintenance of the French horn with emphasis on eliminating the common errors or bad habits which lead to the need for repair work.

unit two

WOODWIND INSTRUMENTS

Chapter 5

GENERAL CARE

The woodwind instruments have one characteristic in common—their intricate key mechanism. While the various tones produced by the brasses depend largely on the performer and a few minimal working parts of the instrument, the production of the various tones by the woodwinds is dependent upon a system of keys, rods, corks, bumpers, and levers, all of which must be in perfect adjustment. Any misalignment can cause bad intonation, poor tone quality, or even no sound at all. From this one can surmise that the majority of woodwind repair work consists of adjusting.

With a young student, the very process of assembling the instrument causes the majority of early repair needs. The neophyte should never attempt to assemble a woodwind instrument without proper instruction. If this instruction, together with advice on the care of the instrument, consumes the time allotted for the student's first lesson, it is time well spent. A separate section in each of the following chapters is devoted to assembling the instruments.

Moisture, too, is a constant problem with the woodwinds, and one almost impossible to eliminate. It can, however, and should, be kept to a minimum.

Moisture appears in the form of condensation from the breath, saliva from the mouth, and from general atmospheric conditions. If water is allowed to impregnate the body of a wooden instrument the body swells and shrinks unevenly because the inside, which has absorbed the greater portion of the water, dries out more slowly than the outside.

Additional stress is created in the wood due to the emulsification and evaporation of the natural oils around the tone holes and in the bore of the instrument. These pressures, thus exerted, can easily cause the wood to crack.

Another reaction will be that the wood will pull away from the metal key posts causing them to become loose. If one of these posts is supporting a needle spring, the tension from the spring can cause the post to turn, thus binding one or more keys and impairing the action. This is one of the first areas to inspect should a key become sluggish or begin to operate improperly.

As the wood dries out and retracts, tenon rings also become loose, the protection they have given to the tenon-receiving area is lost, and cracking can easily occur as pressure is exerted while assembling the instrument. Other effects such as tone holes actually changing shape as the wood shrinks and contracts (causing sudden intonation problems), joints that shrink and will not fit, and steel rods that rust causing keys to bind are additional reasons to impress upon the student the need to protect the instrument by eliminating any exposure to sudden temperature changes, avoiding conditions of excessive (or lack of) humidity, swabbing all sections of the instrument after use, and by the proper application of bore oil.

TOOLS AND ACCESSORIES FOR THE REPAIR AND MAINTENANCE OF THE WOODWIND INSTRUMENTS[1]

BASIC

TOOLS

Small rawhide mallet
Pair of duckbilled (smooth-jawed) pliers
Pair of diagonal cutting pliers (wire cutters)
Pair of needle nose pliers
Pair of roundnose pliers
Small screwdriver (two blades: narrow 1/16", wide 3/32")
Single-edged razor blades
Alcohol burner
Jeweler's anvil
Hard-faced tack hammer
Prick punch, pad slick, feeler gauge, spring hook, screw and rod block[2]

1. See Appendix C for supply companies that will provide catalogs.

2. See pp. 46 and 47 for description and use of these tools.

ACCESSORIES

    Key oil
    Bore oil
    French pad cement
    Stick shellac
    Contact cement
    Emery post washers
    Dental floss or thread
    Emery powder
    Tube of liquid cement
    Piece of cheesecloth or soft linen
    Cork grease
    Sheet cork: 1/64", 1/32", 3/32", 1/8" thickness
    Several pieces of fine sandpaper
    Several pipe cleaners
    Denatured alcohol
    Assortment of needle and flat springs
    Pint of vinegar

SPECIFIC

Clarinet

ACCESSORIES

    Bladder pads sizes 9½, 10, 16, and 16½ (medium thickness) are most common[3]

Oboe

ACCESSORIES

    Bladder pads sizes 7, 11, and 14 (medium thickness) are most common

Flute

TOOLS

    Cleaning rod

ACCESSORIES

    Assorted bladder pads (11½ and 12 without holes; 17½, 18, 18½, and 19 with holes are most common)[3]
    Several dozen paper pad shims or washers

Bassoon

ACCESSORIES

    Assorted tan leather pads (preferably bassoon—saxophone or bass clarinet pads will work in emergencies)

Saxophone

TOOLS

    Mouthpiece brush
    Short flexible brush

ACCESSORIES

    Small assortment of felt bumpers
    Assortment tan leather pads

Screw, Rod, and Spring Block[4]

Use: To hold pivot screws, key rods, and needle springs in a secure and systematic order.

Construction: Pinewood 6" × 3" × 1". Drill four rows of holes: two rows (large) 3/4" deep—about a #32 drill bit; two rows (small) 3/16" deep—about a #46 drill bit.

The large holes are for key rods, the small for pivot screws. The first row (left side) is for the top joint of the instrument, the second for the lower joint or section of the instrument.

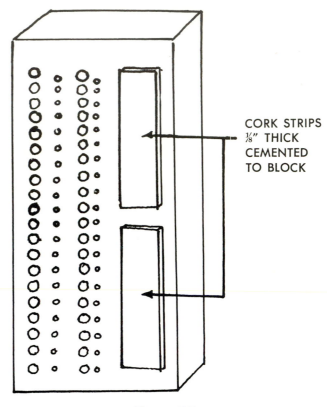

CORK STRIPS ⅛" THICK CEMENTED TO BLOCK

Figure 5.1

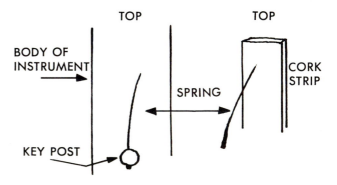

TOP   TOP

BODY OF INSTRUMENT

SPRING

CORK STRIP

KEY POST

Figure 5.2

3. See Appendix F for chart of pad sizes.
4. A block of Styrofoam cut to the approximate same size works as a temporary device.

The needle springs that have been removed are stuck into the cork strips—again, the upper piece for the upper section of the instrument and the bottom strip for the lower section of the instrument. The accepted procedure is to place them pointed and slanted identical to their position when on the instrument.

This provides a retainable, visual image to assist in their replacement.

Prick Punch

Use: A tool to prick a small hole in the edge of bladder pads so trapped moisture or air can escape. It is also used, when inserted into the cardboard back of a pad, as a device to manipulate the pad into position.

Construction: Insert the blunt end of a needle spring or the eye end of a medium-sized needle into a small piece of soft wood. A piece of small dowling works well.

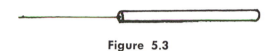

Figure 5.3

Pad Slick

Use: To level, press, or shift bladder pads in the pad cup during the process of seating.

Construction: Although the tool can be purchased through a supply house, the heel of a nail file will work as well.

Feeler Gauge

Use: To locate small leaks on a depressed padded key.

Construction: Glue or tie a thin, pointed slice of cellophane to a wooden match or sliver of wood (piece of a clarinet reed).

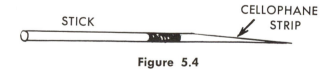

STICK   CELLOPHANE STRIP

Figure 5.4

Spring Hook

Use: To hook up or unhook needle springs.

Construction: Select a #2 or #3 metal (or corresponding plastic) crochet hook and file as shown.

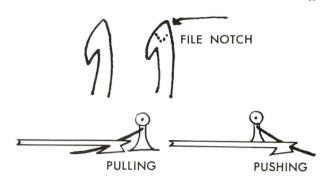

FILE NOTCH

PULLING   PUSHING

Figure 5.5

I. ASSEMBLING

It must first be noted that whenever two sections of a woodwind instrument are assembled they are assembled with a rotating, twisting motion. This reduces the friction as well as the strain on the tenon and the mechanism caused by a tight grip. In addition, on the corked tenons the grain of the cork runs at right angles to the body of the instrument. If the joint is forced on at a right angle to the grain it can easily cause the cork to "chip."

Try to have the hands gripping the instrument as close to the tenon area as possible. This will prevent the instrument from suddenly buckling.

Extreme caution must be observed when assembling an instrument on which the tenon rings are loose. This condition affords little, if any, support to the thin, fragile, female tenon receiver.

Woodwind instruments should always be completely disassembled when put away for any length of time. This is impossible when using some types of cases, such as the old style clarinet cases. These should be discarded and replaced. If an instrument with corked tenons is left assembled for a long time the cork becomes permanently compressed and will eventually develop into a wobbly, leaking joint. There is also danger of the instrument cracking, since it cannot dry out sufficiently if left assembled.

II. CLEANING AND OILING

A. The Body

The acids formed from saliva constitute a major problem for the metal woodwinds. Saliva from the human body contains carbonic acid. Other acids are formed in the mouth, depending on what is eaten or drunk. Because of this, eating candy, chewing gum, or drinking soft drinks should be discouraged before playing. Rinsing the mouth with water will lessen the amount of acids in the saliva.

Moisture is not the sole reason for habitually swabbing out woodwind instruments. Foreign particles such as dirt, tobacco, and food particles work their way into the instrument. Such foreign matter is not only a sanitation hazard, but a serious threat to the intonation of the instrument. Dirt or other foreign particles will cause the throat tones of a clarinet to speak poorly, prevent an oboe or saxophone from overblowing its octaves properly, and cause innumerable other deficiencies in the performing ability of the instrument.

If any form of residue is allowed to build up on the inside of the tone holes of the ring keys the pitch of these tones can be seriously affected. These tone holes should be periodically cleaned with a "Q-Tip" or small wad of cotton wound on a toothpick or wooden match. When the upper joint is swabbed out, care should be taken not to let the weight drop down and hit the register tube which extends into the bore of the instrument. Never wash out the instrument with water. If the bore of a wooden instrument is to be oiled, all pads which normally are closed should have a piece of heavy paper or blotter inserted between them and the tone holes. This will prevent the pads from soaking up oil from the swab or the body of the instrument itself.

Because of the oil in the body of wooden instruments, dust and foreign matter collect very rapidly. This can be removed from between and under the keys with either a small, soft camel's hair brush or a pipe cleaner which has a small amount of oil on it.

One last point to remember is to keep the register key hole clean. This can be done by removing the register key (see Plate IX) and running a pipe cleaner through the breather tube to remove any foreign matter.

B. The Mouthpiece

In swabbing out the instrument after each playing, the mouthpiece often is neglected. This results in a coating of hard saliva residue in the chamber of the mouthpiece. This is highly unsanitary and can cause imperfections in the production of the tone. The correct procedure after each use is to remove the reed, wipe it dry, and place it in a reed holder or container, then swab out the mouthpiece. The weighted swab should not be used here. There is great danger of chipping the tip of the mouth-

piece if the weight is carelessly dropped through the chamber. To swab out the mouthpiece use a regular mouthpiece swab or a soft cloth to run through the hole. If a crust has formed in the chamber, however, never attempt to scrape it out and never place the mouthpiece in hot water. Rather, submerge the mouthpiece (all but the cork) in vinegar for several hours. This will dissolve the crust and it can then be flushed out with cold water and a brush or swab.

NOTE: After swabbing out an instrument it is unwise to keep the wet swab sealed up inside the case with the instrument. The moisture contained in the cloth, chamois, or feather will attack the raw metal of rods, screws, and springs and cause them to corrode.

C. The Key Mechanism

Polishing the keys (or the body of a metal instrument) is not a recommended procedure. It is not disastrous to the life or workability of the instrument if the keys are slightly tarnished. More damage than good usually results from an overzealous student's attempt to keep the instrument bright and shiny. The best advice is to practice prevention. Establish the habit of wiping the keys off with a soft cloth after each use to remove perspiration, which contains many strong acids and alkalies.

All pivot screws, rods, springs, and points of friction should be oiled systematically with key oil or some very light machine oil. This will prevent rusting, minimize wear, and assure efficient key action. Apply the oil with a needle or toothpick and wipe off all excess. The frequency of this operation will depend upon the climate, age of the instrument, and amount of use.

D. The Pads

As a matter of process, the pads on a woodwind instrument will absorb oil from the body. This in turn will pick up dust and other foreign matter resulting in a sticky pad. These may be cleaned temporarily by (1) placing a dollar bill (which is absorbent, rough-textured, pliable, and yet strong) between the pad and the tone hole, and then (2) pressing the pad down and withdrawing the bill. Repeated several times it will clean both the pad and the rim of the tone hole.

A more lasting and efficient procedure is to clean the pad with one end of a pipe cleaner dampened with denatured alcohol. The dry end of the cleaner is used to remove any excess alcohol on the pad immediately. After this has been done, another pipe cleaner with a very small amount of key oil on it is run over the pad lightly. This latter step is essential because the alcohol will dry out the skin of the pad and cause it to crack if some of the oil is not replaced.

III. REPAIRS AND MAINTENANCE

A. The Body

1. Cracks

Some manufacturers claim that only 10 percent of the actual grenadilla wood purchased is used for the bodies of clarinets. The other 90 percent is lost in the process of curing, treating, cutting, and sawing. This, it seems, should result in as near perfect a piece of wood as is humanly possible; yet, as before stated, no wooden instrument is guaranteed against cracking.

If the instrument does crack it is not a great tragedy. Many fine, expensive old clarinets used today have cracked and been pinned several times without impairing their looks or tone. The danger lies in failure to have the crack taken care of immediately and in not selecting a competent repairman to do the job.

As soon as a crack is noticed, it should be marked. This can be done with a dab of fingernail polish, some form of tape or even a pencil mark. This precaution is taken because by the time the instrument reaches a repair shop the wood may have swollen and closed the crack completely, thus making it difficult for the repairman to find the crack or determine its extent.

There are two methods of repairing a crack. One is to screw steel pins diagonally through the wood to pull the wood together, thus closing the crack and holding it shut. This is called "pinning." The other method, called "banding," is a process of shrinking a silver or aluminum band around the body over the crack, obtaining the same results as the foregoing. This latter procedure is rather expensive. Pinning is more economical and, if done correctly, will prove just as good if not better than banding. Neither, however, will assure a crack from reopening.

There is very little danger of a bassoon's cracking. This is due to several factors. The wood is maple and more pliable than grenadilla. Both the inside and the outside are treated to resist moisture; the outside is sealed and varnished while the bore is shellacked.

On any good bassoon, the tenor joint and the tenor side of the boot are also lined with rubber to prevent moisture collecting. (This is one factor to keep in mind when buying the instrument.) Because of the condition of the bore and the lining of the tenor joint, the bore of the bassoon is never oiled.

2. Loose Tenon Rings

As a wooden instrument dries out, the wood shrinks. This process will cause rings and posts to become loose to the extent that a tenon ring may drop off completely. The tenon ring is a metal band which fits around the rim of the tenon receiver (see Plate IX). Because the body is quite thin at this point, the metal ring acts as a reinforcement. If it becomes loose, the protection it offers is of no value.

There are two methods of replacing a loose tenon ring. One is to have the ring shrunk with a compressing device. The other is to have a shim of cheesecloth or thin linen placed under the ring. The latter is simpler, costs less, is quicker, and generally preferred. The reason for its preference is that, if the ring is shrunk on, it does not leave any expansion room if and when the wood returns to its normal state. With the use of the cloth shim expansion is possible.

The procedure to replace a loose tenon ring with a cloth shim is as follows.

Materials needed:

1. Strip of cheesecloth or thin linen about three inches square
2. Razor blade
3. Small rubber, plastic, or rawhide mallet
4. Tube of liquid pad cement

Procedure:

1. Remove the loose ring. If it does not fall off, but is loose enough to cause a vibrating buzz when the instrument is played, insert the blade of a table knife or jackknife under the edge of the ring and pry it upward by twisting the blade.

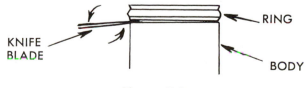

Figure 5.6

The ring often is slightly beveled, so take care to replace it the same way it came off.

2. Scrape the inside of the ring to remove the old glue and clean the ring groove on the body.

Figure 5.7

3. Spread a thin coat of pad cement on the ring groove.

4. Stretch the cloth for the shim over the end of the body.

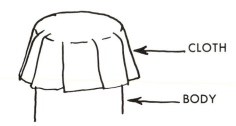

Figure 5.8

5. Replace the ring over the tenon and tap it down. DO NOT tap it all the way on but leave about 1/32″ clearance. This allows room to cut the surplus cloth away without leaving any loose fringes.

6. Take the razor blade and cut away the surplus cloth from around the bottom of the ring.

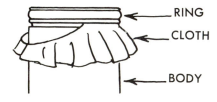

Figure 5.9

7. Next tap the ring all the way on and cut away the cloth that covers the hole.

If the bottom bell ring becomes loose there is no simple way to tighten it. This must be done by a repairman using proper equipment.

A loose tenon ring on an oboe is very uncommon. The reasons for this are that the rings are more securely attached to the body of the instrument than those of other woodwinds, and that the posts of the key mechanism are soldered onto the tenon rings, making the rings a part of the key assemblage.

3. Loose Posts

The post on wooden instruments are screwed into the body of the instrument. If the wood around the threads shrinks, the post will become loose and bind the rod or key it is holding. Some manufacturers have installed pins or lock plates on the more vital posts to prevent them from turning. Many instruments, however, especially the cheaper or student line models, lack this feature.

If a post becomes loose, it can be tightened quite easily with any one of three following methods. Regardless of which method is used, the first step is to remove the key or rod connected to the post. If the post is in a position where several keys must be removed and the operation appears to be quite extensive, it is best to leave it to an experienced repairman. If the post is one that is easily accessible, the second step is to check to see if the post can be screwed out of the body. If a spring in the post prevents this it must be removed. (See section on removing and replacing needle springs in this chapter.)

Materials needed: (First method)
1. Emery powder or a piece of fine sandpaper
2. Duckbilled pliers or any smooth-jawed pliers
3. Small screwdriver

Procedure 1:
1. With the pliers, loosen the post about two full turns.
2. Spread a small amount of emery powder or grit, scraped from a piece of fine sandpaper, under the base of the post.
3. Screw the post back to its original position.
4. Remount the rod or key.

Materials needed: (Second method)
1. Dental floss or thread
2. Liquid pad cement
3. Duckbilled pliers or any smooth-jawed pliers
4. Small screwdriver

Procedure 2:

1. With the pliers, remove the post completely.
2. Wind the screw threads of the post with dental floss or thread.
3. Place a small amount of pad cement in the post hole.
4. Screw the post back to its original position and allow it to stand for about an hour to let the cement harden.
5. Remount the rod or key.

Materials needed: (Third method)

1. Emery washers which can be purchased from a repair shop
2. Duckbilled pliers or any smooth-jawed pliers
3. Small screwdriver

Procedure 3:

1. With the pliers, remove the post completely.
2. Slip the washer over the threaded area of the post, making sure the emery side is facing down.

EMERY WASHER

Figure 5.10

3. Replace the post in the hole and screw it back to its original position.
4. Remount the rod and key.

This third method is the most satisfactory emergency repair, as well as being the least time-consuming.

There are two methods used by repairmen. One is to drill a small hole through the edge of the base part of the post and into the wood of the body. A small pin or screw is then inserted in this hole to anchor the post to the body. The other method is to remove the post and fit and solder a threaded shim over the old threads, which have been filed smooth. The post hole in the body is then rethreaded with a tap and the post screwed back in place.

4. Tenon Recorking—Permanent

If an instrument is not completely disassembled each time it is put away, the corks on the tenons will become permanently compressed and cause a wobbly, leaky joint. A loose joint also can develop simply from continual use and wear.

The actual process of replacing a tenon cork is as follows (permanent).

Materials needed:

1. Sheet of cork, either 1/16″ or 3/32″ thick
2. Stick shellac or contact cement
3. Teaspoon with a flat, square-tipped handle
4. Alcohol burner
5. Several 3/4″ strips of sandpaper
6. Razor blade

Procedure:

1. Remove any keys which extend down over the tenon.
2. Remove thoroughly all of the old cork and shellac from the tenon.
3. Measure the width of the groove on the tenon and cut a strip of cork the same width. Be sure the cork strip is cut to go with the grain, and that the strip is long enough to go completely around the tenon with about an inch overlap.
4. With the razor blade, bevel one end of the strip.

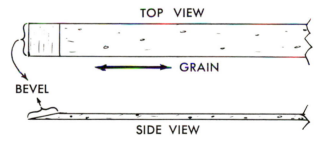

TOP VIEW

GRAIN

BEVEL

SIDE VIEW

*If contact cement used, apply to this side and to the top face of the bevel.

Figure 5.11

5. Hold the stick shellac over the flame of the alcohol burner. When it becomes quite soft, remove it immediately and smear a dab of the shellac on an area of the tenon to be corked. Do this at several spots around the tenon.
6. Heat the tip of the handle of the spoon and apply it to a section of shellac on the tenon. This will melt a portion of the shellac. Immediately press the beveled end of the cork strip (with the beveled edge up) into the

Figure 5.12

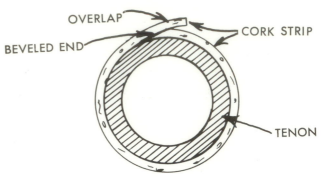

Figure 5.14

melted shellac and hold it in place with the thumb until the cement hardens. Be especially sure that the edges of the cork are well cemented to the tenon.

10. With a strip of sandpaper, strop the corked tenon to remove the excess cork.

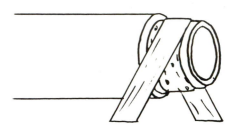

Figure 5.15

11. Sand a bevel on the edges of the cork so they will not snag and tear when the sections are tried together (see Fig. 5.16).

Figure 5.13

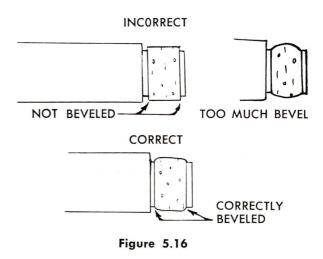

Figure 5.16

7. Reheat the spoon handle and press it under the cork to melt more of the shellac. When the shellac is melted press more of the cork strip down and hold it until the shellac hardens (see Fig. 5.13).

8. Repeat this procedure until the entire tenon is covered. Be sure to overlap the strip up over the beveled end.

9. Cut off the surplus strip of cork and chip away any surplus shellac that has oozed out.

12. From time to time try fitting the two sections together. Each time an attempt is made, however, the newly corked tenon must be well greased. If it is too large to permit a fit, the

grease must be wiped off and the tenon stropped again with the sandpaper strip.

13. When a proper fit is attained reassemble any keys which had to be removed.

Instead of stick shellac, a contact cement may be used. Follow steps 1 through 4 then apply contact cement to the tenon and to the underside of the strip of cork (see Fig. 5.11),. allow to dry for the required time (see directions on container), and fit in place (see Fig. 5.14). Then proceed with steps 9 through 13.

5. Tenon Recorking—Emergency

If for some reason it is not possible or practical to completely recork the tenon, there are several emergency techniques which will suffice until there is time available to either send the instrument to a repair shop or recork the tenon properly.

One process is to coat the cork with cork grease and rotate the tenon over a small flame such as an alcohol lamp, cigarette lighter, or match.

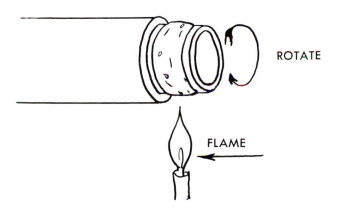

ROTATE

FLAME

Figure 5.17

Care must be taken to keep the tenon moving constantly to avoid burning the cork. The combination of grease plus heat will cause the cork to swell, thus providing a temporary tight-fitting joint. This procedure can be repeated when the need arises, though eventually it will lose its effectiveness.

Another method is to wind the loose joint with dental floss.[1] This can be used even to replace the entire cork on the tenon.

A third method requires the use of several sizes of plastic rings, which, after the old cork has been cleaned off, can be slipped over the tenon and used

in place of the cork. These first were used on some new clarinets to take the place of the corks on the tenons, but did not prove as satisfactory as cork and are now used more for emergency repairs.

On a new clarinet the joints often are quite tight and, as mentioned previously, the corks should be thoroughly greased before the joints are fitted together. If it still is impossible to fit the joints or if they fit very tightly, the cause can be that the very end of the tenon (wood) has expanded. In this case the binding is only noticed when the tenons are completely joined. Inspect this area carefully for any signs of wear or rubbing. If this is not the case, or if it is obvious that the tenon cork is too large, it may be sanded down and the joint tried again. This sanding is done by taking a strip of fine sandpaper one-half inch wide and stropping the cork tenon.

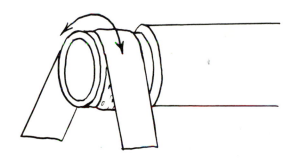

Figure 5.18

B. The Mechanism

1. Loose Screws or Rods

Often, due simply to the constant action of a key, the set screw or rod will begin to work its way out of a post. This can be prevented by burring the post hole into the slot of the screw or rod.

Procedure:

1. Take a sharp metal object or small screwdriver and place it against the post near the slot of the screw or rod and strike it with a mallet. This will cause a burr to protrude into the slot of the screw or rod thus anchoring it and preventing it from turning or unwinding by itself.

1. Dental floss, because of its texture and coating, will compress itself and form a smooth, compact surface.

Figure 5.19

2. Springs

Almost all the key action on the woodwind instruments is the result of a series of springs—either needle or flat—properly placed and properly tensioned. Often, because of a sudden jar or mishandling, a spring can become unhooked. Should a key fail to function properly, many problems can be eliminated if this area is inspected first.

If an inspection of a flat spring does not reveal the reason for its sluggishness, inspect the small metal plate (on the body of the instrument) on which the foot of the spring rests and slides. Rust collected on this plate or on the foot of the spring will prevent the key from operating properly. Both the spring and the small metal plate should periodically receive a drop of oil.

Improper key action can also be caused by a weak or broken spring. These should be replaced.

If the spring is a flat spring, simply remove the key, unscrew the small screw that holds the spring, remove, and replace with one that is as similar (length and strength) as possible.

The removal and replacement of a needle spring is as follows.

Materials needed:

1. Wire cutter pliers
2. Roundnose pliers

Procedure:

1. Remove any keys necessary to expose the post and spring completely. Remember always that the spring must be pushed back through the post, never pulled through it.
2. With one hand use the wire cutters to grip the spring about 1/4″ from the post. With

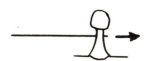

Figure 5.20

the other hand use the roundnose pliers to force the spring out (see Fig. 5.21).

To replace the spring, push it through the hole in the post and wedge it in place, using the wire cutters (see Fig. 5.22).

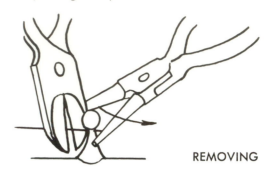

REMOVING

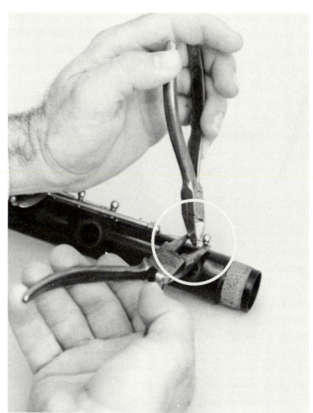

Figure 5.21

If a new needle spring must be installed to replace a worn or broken one, proceed as follows.

Materials needed:

1. Assortment of needle springs
2. Hard-faced tack hammer
3. Alcohol lamp

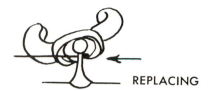

REPLACING

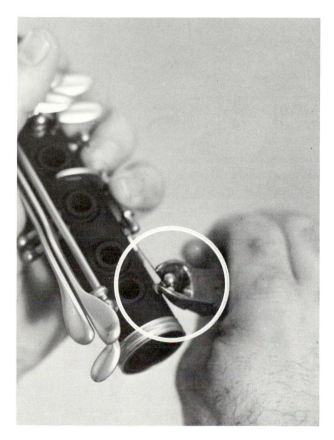

Figure 5.22

4. Jeweler's anvil
5. Wire cutters

Procedure:

1. Select a spring that will fit snugly into the hole.
2. Place the key which the spring is to operate on the instrument so that the length can be determined. The pointed end of the spring should reach about 1/4″ beyond the hook on the key.
3. If the spring needs to be shortened, note the desired length, remove it from the post, and stick one end into a piece of wood or cork. Hold on to the other end while it is cut with the wire cutters. The steel in the spring is

Figure 5.23

very brittle and will "fly away" if not held firmly.

4. Expose the very tip of the thick end to a flame until it turns a straw color—do not overheat or all the temper in the spring will be lost.
5. Quickly lay the tip of the spring on the jeweler's anvil and hammer a small wedge on the end.
6. Follow the previously mentioned process of replacement.
7. Once the spring has been secured in place, it must be properly tensioned.

NOTE: If the pad cup is to remain open, bend the spring toward the hole (see Fig. 5.24, A). If it is to remain closed, bend the spring away from the tone hole (see Fig. 5.24, B).

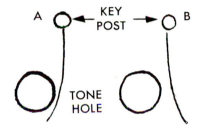

Figure 5.24

8. Replace the key and check for strength and response.

3. Key Recorking

Corks are cemented on the keys for two reasons: to eliminate noise and for adjustment purposes. Regardless of which factor is involved, if a cork breaks off a key the outcome is certain to impair the playing ability of the instrument in some way. Emergency repairs of this nature therefore are quite frequent.

Materials needed:

1. Cork (sheets of 1/64″, 1/32″, and 3/32″ are the most common)

2. Razor blade
3. Stick shellac or contact cement
4. Alcohol burner or cigarette lighter
5. Piece of fine sandpaper
6. Wet cloth
7. Small screwdriver

Procedure:

1. Remove the key concerned from the body of the clarinet.

2. With the razor blade, scrape off the old cork and glue.

3. Using the old cork as a pattern, select the correct thickness of cork and cut a piece larger than needed from the sheet. If the old cork is lost, compare the key with one on another clarinet, or simply guess.

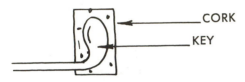

Figure 5.25

4. Heat the key, applying the flame to the side opposite that on which the cork is to be applied, and at the same time apply the stick shellac to the area to be corked. Smear a thin coat over the required area. Use only enough heat to melt the stick shellac.

5. Remove the key from the flame and press the cork onto the key firmly. Do not press too hard, however, or the shellac will be squeezed out. If a wet cloth is used to set the key on, the shellac will harden more quickly.

6. If a wet cloth is used the shellac will be set in about ten seconds. The next procedure is to trim away the excess cork with the razor

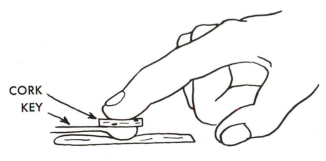

Figure 5.26

blade. In doing so, always cut toward the key rather than away from it so as not to tear the cork from the key. Make all cuts slanting, thus leaving neat, beveled edges.

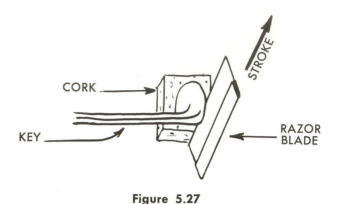

Figure 5.27

7. The last step is to smooth the beveled surfaces with sandpaper.

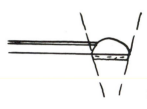

Figure 5.28

8. Check to make sure the new cork allows the key to operate properly. If it is one which regulates the opening of a tone hole, a small amount may have to be sanded or cut off to allow the cup to raise to the proper height (at least 1/8″).

NOTE: This same operation can be done using contact cement instead of heat and stick shellac. Avoid, however, liquid shellac (in tubes). This is not only messy, but much time is lost waiting for it to dry and harden.

CAUTION: Some keys on cheaper instruments are made of "pot metal" (identified by embossed numbers on each key). This has a very low melting point and extreme care should be taken when working with them. This includes the following process for pad replacing.

4. Pads

At present woodwind pads are made of a number of different materials—fish skin and felt, plastic, leather, cork, and even rubber. Each type, except rubber, has its merits and each type has its place. The most suitable for the wooden soprano clarinet is the bladder or fish skin type, although a leather or cork pad is recommended on the register key. The sharp rim of the speaker tube can quickly cut through a fish skin pad. This type of pad is also recommended on the G♯ key. This is an area where a great deal of saliva collects, and a fish skin pad here will rot very quickly. Although cork and leather pads will outlast the bladder type, they are very noisy, especially the cork, and will not "seat" as well as the skin type. Plastic pads are presently in the experimental stage. If plastic proves satisfactory it will provide pads that not only seat well, but are highly durable. Rubber was strictly an experiment that failed and is undesirable for any type of woodwind instrument. Leather pads work best on the bass and alto clarinets and all metal clarinets.

5. Pad Replacing—Bladder-type

Materials needed:

1. Assorted bladder pads
2. Stick of French pad cement
3. Prick punch
4. Pad slick
5. Feeler gauge
6. Alcohol lamp
7. Spring hook
8. Small screwdriver

Procedure:

1. Remove the key from the body of the instrument. (This step is not a must, but it is preferred because it allows a thorough cleaning

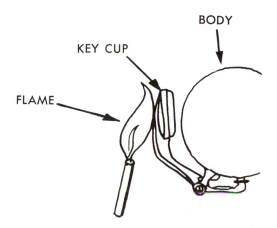

Figure 5.29

of the pad cup and eliminates the danger of burning the body of the clarinet and/or other pads and corks. If the key is left on the instrument, it is raised so the cup is up and away from the body as far as possible. The cup is then exposed to the edge of the flame to soften the glue so the pad can be removed with the prick punch.)

Figure 5.30

2. If the key is removed, hold it pad up over the flame to melt the old cement and loosen the pad.
3. With the prick punch, lift out the old pad.
4. Clean out the pad cup thoroughly.
5. Select the correct size pad. If possible use the old one as a pattern. The pad should not be oversized or it may hit the sides of the tone hole and not seat properly. Likewise, it should not be undersized or it may not cover the tone hole properly. The thickness of the pad must be considered also. A pad which is too thick is as difficult to seat as one which is too thin.

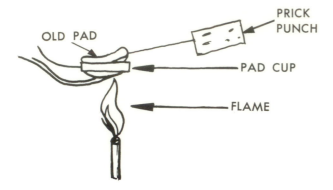

Figure 5.31

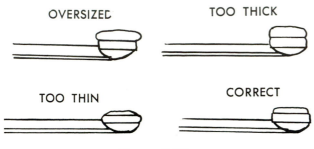

Figure 5.32

(Some repairmen prefer to use a pad that is quite thin and then float it in with pad cement. This method has much merit but is not recommended for the amateur.)

6. The next step is to prick a hole in the edge of the pad with the needle. This will provide a release valve for any moisture that collects during the seating of the pad and/or during its use. Failure to do this will result in pads actually blowing up like balloons from the moisture trapped inside the bladder skin.

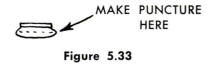

Figure 5.33

7. Insert the needle into the side of the cardboard washer on the back of the pad. This will hold it nicely while the cement is applied.
8. Hold the stick of French pad cement over the flame until it begins to melt, then quickly smear a small dab on the back of the pad.
9. Again heat the pad cup of the key over the flame.

Figure 5.34

10. When it is quite warm—but not hot—remove it from the flame and place the pad in the cup.

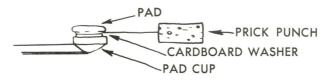

Figure 5.35

11. Remove the prick punch and press the pad in place with the pad slick. Make sure it is even all the way around. If any cement oozes out, let it harden then chip it off. Do not try to wipe it off while it is hot because this will only smear the cement over the key and the pad itself.
12. Replace the key on the instrument.

Replacing a pad on a bass or alto clarinet is basically the same procedure. If a pad falls out of a key on such an instrument it can be replaced by simply putting a small amount of liquid pad cement on the back of the pad and replacing it in the pad cup. This is not a permanent repair, and the pad probably will not be seated properly, but it is an emergency procedure which will last until the instrument can be taken care of properly by a repairman.

The next step—seating the pad—is a complete operation in itself and so is treated separately.

6. Pad Seating

Materials needed:
1. Feeler gauge
2. Pad slick
3. Alcohol lamp
4. Pipe cleaner

Procedure:
1. Insert the tip of the feeler gauge between the pad and the rim of the tone hole. Depress the key lightly and slowly withdraw the gauge. If

the pad is seating properly at this point there will be a noticeable "drag" on the feeler gauge as it is removed. If there is a light drag, the pad is seating, but poorly; if there is no drag, the pad is not seating. This should be repeated at several points around the pad. This not only will determine whether the pad is leaking, but also will indicate the exact spot.

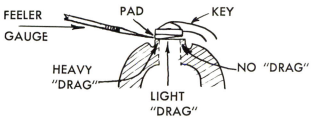

Figure 5.36

2. The next step now is to shift the pad so the drag on the feeler gauge is even all around the tone hole. The key should not be removed from the instrument while shifting the pad, although other keys may have to be removed for the sake of accessibility.

3. Expose the backside of the cup to the edge of the flame for about three or four seconds, or long enough to soften the cement inside. The cement should never be heated to the point that it will run. Be careful also that the flame does not come in direct contact with the pad or the body of the instrument.

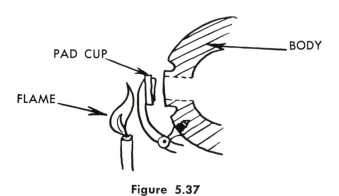

Figure 5.37

4. When the cement has softened, insert the pad slick between the pad and tone hole and shift it to the desired position.

5. After the pad has been shifted, test it again with the feeler gauge. If necessary, shift the

Figure 5.38

pad again until the drag on the feeler gauge is even all around the pad.

6. If time allows and a bladder pad has been used, dampen the skin of the pad with a wet pipe cleaner.

7. Use a rubber band or a strip of cloth and tie the key down firmly. Allow it to stand two to three hours. This will press a permanent seat in the pad that will further assure a leakproof fit.

Some makes of soprano clarinets do not have a tone hole seat for the C♯-G♯ key. There is only a hole drilled into the body of the instrument and the pad must be seated to this smooth, curved surface. If a pad must be replaced on this key the pad first must be bent to conform to the curve of the body. The quickest and simplest way is to bend the pad over a round object such as a pencil. The process of seating the pad is then followed with special attention given the last step, which is dampening the pad, tying it down, and letting it dry. This latter process is a must for this type of key.

SPECIAL TIPS

A. Stuck Swab

The first thing that wears out with a "pull through" type of swab is the cord. Unfortunately, it invariably breaks when the swab is being pulled through the bore of the instrument.

Usually this happens when the swab is in the top joint of the clarinet at the point where the speaker tube extends into the bore. The frantic student's first action will be to grab a pencil and begin jamming the swab first one way then the other, eventually compressing it into a small, tight wad which is next to impossible to remove.

The first rule to remember is not to attempt to move the swab out of the instrument in the direction it was headed, but rather to work it backwards out of the bore. This can be done by inserting a long-bladed screwdriver, a stiff wire or a buttonhook up into the bore. Care must be taken here not to scratch or gouge the sides of the bore. The screwdriver or wire is then gently pushed into the swab and twisted until the swab winds onto it. This can be felt. Once the swab has wound itself on the wire or screwdriver, it can be slowly withdrawn. This operation may have to be repeated several times before the swab is removed from the bore. If the swab cannot be removed, the instrument should be taken to a repairman who has the proper tool and can extract the swab in a matter of minutes.

B. Keys and Locks

Many new instruments come complete with a screwdriver and a set of keys to lock the case. These are a headache to many a band director. The screwdriver is a constant temptation to the young student who thinks he can adjust his own instrument. The outcome is almost always disastrous. If the student has a set of keys it is best to have him leave one with the band director. In fact, directors are wise to keep several such keys—most of them are alike—on hand for forgetful students.

Chapter 6

THE CLARINETS

PLATE IX—SOPRANO CLARINET

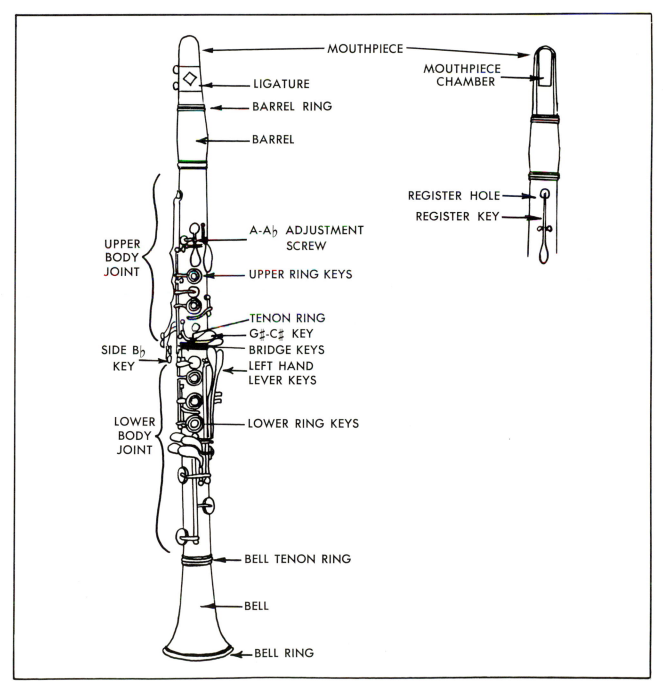

MOUTHPIECE

LIGATURE

BARREL RING

BARREL

MOUTHPIECE
CHAMBER

UPPER
BODY
JOINT

A-A♭ ADJUSTMENT
SCREW

UPPER RING KEYS

REGISTER HOLE

REGISTER KEY

TENON RING

G♯-C♯ KEY

SIDE B♭
KEY

BRIDGE KEYS

LEFT HAND
LEVER KEYS

LOWER
BODY
JOINT

LOWER RING KEYS

BELL TENON RING

BELL

BELL RING

PLATE X—BASS CLARINET

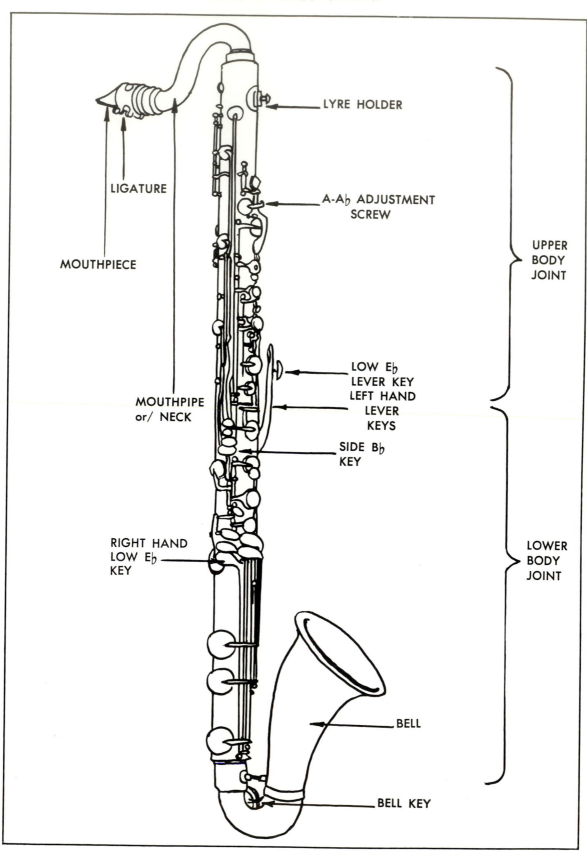

LYRE HOLDER

A-Ab ADJUSTMENT
SCREW

LIGATURE

MOUTHPIECE

UPPER
BODY
JOINT

LOW Eb
LEVER KEY
LEFT HAND
LEVER
KEYS

MOUTHPIPE
or/ NECK

SIDE Bb
KEY

RIGHT HAND
LOW Eb
KEY

LOWER
BODY
JOINT

BELL

BELL KEY

I. ASSEMBLING

The first step in assembling the clarinet is to see that all tenons are liberally coated with cork grease. The grease not only will assure an easy fit and preserve the life of the cork, but also will prevent "frozen" tenons and the damaged keys and rods that result from efforts to untwist the stuck sections.

A. Soprano Clarinet

For practical purposes the barrel is joined to the top of the upper joint first for no other reason than to protect the tenon of this section during the rest of the assembly. The next step, which is both the most precarious and most important, is to put the upper and lower body sections together.

The danger here lies with the protruding bridge keys. These are the two small levers that join the mechanism of the lower body joint to that of the top body joint.

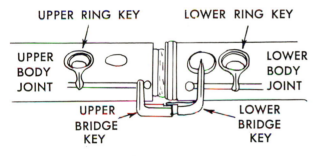

Figure 6.1

Figure 6.2

The correct procedure to prevent damage to these keys is to grip the upper body joint around the ring keys. This will automatically raise the upper bridge key. The lower body joint must be grasped so that the lower bridge key remains down. The two sections are then joined with short twisting movements. When the two sections are correctly joined, the upper bridge key overlaps the bottom bridge key.

The next step is to join on the bell section. Except for the ligature and reed, the mouthpiece, because of its fragility, is the last section to be assembled. The hole in the tone chamber should line up with the register key (see Plate IX).

When assembling the mouthpiece ligature and reed, it is advisable to place the ligature on the mouthpiece first and then slip the reed under it. If the procedure is reversed, the chances of snagging

the reed with the ligature are very great, especially when attempted by young students.

B. Alto and Bass Clarinet

The assembling of the bass or alto clarinet is very similar to that of the soprano clarinet. The bodies of some bass and alto clarinets are of one piece. If this is not the case, the two body joints should be assembled first. Again, as with the soprano clarinet, precaution must be observed so as not to damage the bridge keys. Many bass and alto clarinets have two sets of these keys which must be joined. After the two body sections are joined the bell is added. A key arrangement similar to the bridge key levers is used here also and must be assembled properly.

The body bridge key must go under the spatula of the bell key.

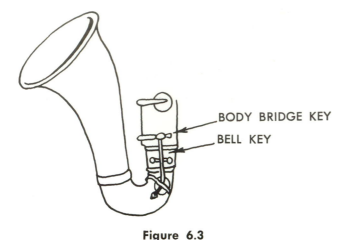

Figure 6.3

The mouthpiece, or neck, is the next to be assembled. Here, too, many bass and alto clarinets use bridge keys to join the octave mechanism to the body keys. The last to be assembled are the mouthpiece, ligature, and reed in that order.

Owing to the various makes, styles, and intricate structures, a discussion of the contrabass clarinets has been omitted. However, all previous instructions and suggestions are adaptable to and encouraged in the assembling of these instruments.

II. COMMON ADJUSTMENT PROBLEMS

Most adjustment problems are best left to the deft fingers of a good repairman. There are several which occur frequently, however, and are easily remedied.

A. Bridge Mechanism

The most frequent, but least harmful, of the key systems to get out of order is the bridge mechanism. It is the most common because of the exposed keys and the method in which the clarinet is assembled.[1] It is the least harmful because the bridge mechanism

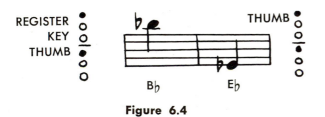

Figure 6.4

controls the auxiliary fingerings for only two tones, B♭ and E♭.

If a clarinet fails to sound these tones, the bridge keys should be checked in the following manner.

Materials needed:
1. Feeler gauge
2. Duckbilled pliers or any pliers with smooth jaws

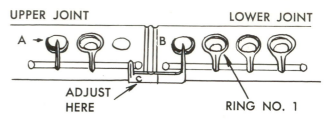

Figure 6.5

Procedure:

With a feeler gauge:
1. Check to make certain both pads (A and B) are seating properly individually.
2. Press ring no. 1 down with the same amount of pressure used when playing the instrument.
3. Check with the feeler gauge to see which pad (A or B) is not seating properly when only ring no. 1 is pressed down.
4. If pad B is not seating, bend lever C up. If pad A is not seating, bend lever C down. Before the lever is bent, rotate the joints so that the levers are free of one another and there is room to work with the pliers.
5. Each time after a lever is bent check both pads with the feeler gauge. When the system is in perfect adjustment and ring no. 1 is depressed, both pads will produce an even drag on the feeler gauge.

B. Side B♭ Key

If a clarinet fails to produce more than one or two tones, the trouble usually can be found in the keys of the upper joint. The first thing to look for is a key with the pad missing. If this is not the case, look for a bent key, which in the majority of cases will be the side B♭ (see Plate IX) since this key is

---

1. The mechanism on the bass and alto clarinet is almost identical.

very exposed, especially when the instrument is disassembled.

C. A-A♭ Combination

On most models of clarinets there is a small screw located on top of the A♭ key. This screw is used to adjust the action between the A and the A♭ key. If the screw is turned in too far it will not allow the A♭ key to seat. The same thing will result if the pad on the A key swells slightly.

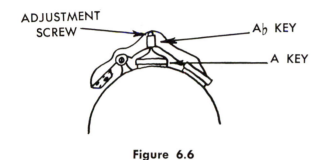

Figure 6.6

With the use of a feeler gauge the A♭ key can be tested to see if it is seating. If it is not, the adjustment screw should be loosened as far as it will go and then the pad retested. When the A♭ key is seating firmly, the screw can be turned back until there is only a very small amount of play between the adjustment screw and the A key.

D. Left-Hand Lever Keys

Located on the lower joint on the left-hand side are two long lever keys (see Plate IX). These operate the keys which produce the low E and F♯ and the middle B and C♯. The point at which they join is silenced with small pieces of fish skin. If this skin is lost or wears out the action is noisy and annoying although not necessarily detrimental to the production of the tones. To replace these silencers the following procedure is taken.

Materials needed:

1. Small screwdriver
2. A few old bladder (fish skin) pads
3. Key oil

Procedure:

1. Remove the two left-hand lever keys.
2. Cut two square pieces of fish skin (one for

each key) measuring about 1/4″ from an old clarinet pad.
3. Dampen the squares with the tip of the tongue and place them over the holes in the E-B and F♯-C♯ keys.
4. Dip both of the pins, located on the end of the lever keys, in key oil and push them into place in the holes of the E-B and F♯-C♯ keys.

Replace the rods that hold the left-hand lever keys.

III. SPECIAL TIPS

A. Intonation

One section used for tuning the clarinet is the barrel which is moved in or out from the upper body joint. If, when the barrel is on all the way and the individual is using a correct embouchure, the clarinet still plays flat, the barrel should be cut down, thus raising the pitch. This naturally must be done by a skilled, well-equipped repairman. The whole clarinet need not be sent to the shop, however, only the mouthpiece and barrel, since the cutting is done from the top of the barrel. Never allow more than the width of the top tenon ring to be cut off or the throat tones of the instrument will be seriously out of tune.

B. Testing for Pad Leaks

If an instrument blows "stuffy" and/or fails to respond in rapid passages, a leaking pad is almost always the cause. Pad leaks usually can be traced to one of two things: either the pad is not seated properly, or the skin has become old and broken or torn by abuse or an accident.

To locate the exact pad or pads that are leaking, one joint at a time is tested by the following process.

Procedure:

1. Cover all the holes with the fingers and/or by depressing the keys.
2. Seal one end of the section with either a cork or the palm of the hand.
3. When this is done it is best to stand in front of a mirror so that all keys can be viewed.
4. Blow smoke into the open end.
5. Locate the leak by observing where the smoke seeps out.
6. Examine the pad and determine whether it must be replaced or simply reseated. If the

pad is to be replaced, see the section on pads in Chapter 5.

C. Stuck Tenons

In spite of precautionary measures, the joints of the soprano clarinet sometimes become frozen together. This seldom happens to the middle joint but more often to the mouthpiece, barrel, or bell, especially if they are left assembled when the instrument is put away. If this does happen, the joints often can be separated by inserting the blade of a sturdy jack-knife into the crack between the two pieces.

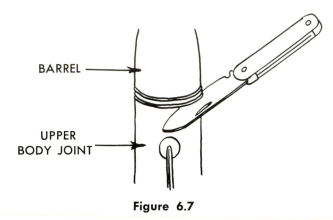

Figure 6.7

Once the blade has been worked into the crack, the knife is twisted, thus prying the sections apart. This operation should be repeated at several places around the joint. The joint need be separated only approximately one-sixteenth of an inch, since this is sufficient to break the seal. The joint then can be separated by hand.

D. Binding Keys

When a pivot screw has been removed and replaced, the key it holds may suddenly fail to function.

As a key that is being held by a pivot screw spins back and forth during normal use, the screw forms its own unique little groove (seat). When the screw is removed and replaced, the point may seat in a dif-

ferent position than it had originally taken. This temporary misplacement will cause a key to bind and the point of the pivot screw must be reseated.

Materials needed:
1. Wide-bladed screwdriver
2. Rawhide mallet
3. Key oil

Procedure:
1. Place the blade of the screwdriver against the cup bar or lever bar close to the bound pivot screw and tap firmly with the rawhide mallet.

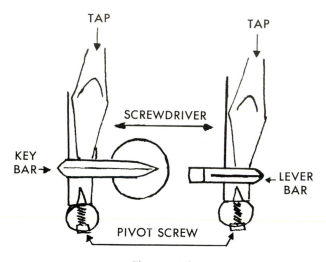

Figure 6.8

This will drive the rod into the point of the pivot screw and reseat the screw.
2. Add a drop of key oil to the pivot area.

This technique will also often relieve a key that is bound due to some flexing of the wood due to shrinkage or swelling.

If, after one or two attempts of tapping the bar against the pivot screw, the problem has not been remedied, inspect other areas for the possible cause, such as a bent key, rusted rod or pivot screw, or loose spring.

IV. INSTRUMENT INSPECTION CHECK SHEET

Clarinets

Instrument. . . . .   Serial Number.   Make. . . . .

School. . . . .   Private. . . . .   School or Manufacturer's Number . . . .

Finish. . . . .   Other Notations . . . .

| | Needs | |
| O.K. | Attention | |

MOUTHPIECE

1. Does the mouthpiece have a reed cap?
2. Is the tip of the mouthpiece chipped?
3. Is the cork in good condition and does the mouthpiece fit the barrel properly without any play?
4. Does the mouthpiece need cleaning?
5. Is the ligature in good condition (any screws missing)?
6. (Other comments)

BODY

1. Are there any signs of cracking?
2. Are there any chipped tone holes?
3. Do any of the tone holes need cleaning?
4. Are any of the tenons broken or badly chipped?
5. Is the thumb rest loose?
6. Are there any loose tenon or bell rings?
7. Are the tenons well corked so that there is no play when the sections are fitted together?
8. Does the wood look dried out and in need of oil?
9.

KEY MECHANISM

1. Are there any bent or broken keys (check especially the bridge keys)?
2. Are there any pivot screws or key rods missing?
3. Do all keys operate freely and easily?
4. Are the corks missing from any of the keys?
5. Is the key system overly noisy, due to missing corks or lack of oil?
6.

PADS

1. Are there any loose or missing pads?
2. Are there any pads in bad condition (torn, hard, brittle, seating improperly, sticking)?
3.

CASE

1. Does the case need repair (hinges, locks, or handle)?
2. Does the instrument fit securely in the case?
3. Are there any accessories lying loose in the case which can damage the instrument?
4.

OTHER COMMENTS

Date . . . .

(signature)

V. CLASS PROJECT SHEET

Clarinets

A. Know the names of the various parts of the instrument.

B. Be able to perform the following operations using the correct procedures, techniques, and tools.

1. Refit a loose tenon ring using a cloth shim
2. Refit a loose post using:

    a. emery powder or grit from a piece of sandpaper
    b. dental floss
    c. emery washer

3. Remove a needle spring and replace it with a new one
4. Perform emergency measures to remedy a loose tenon using:

    a. cork grease and heat
    b. dental floss

5. Completely recork and fit a tenon
6. Separate two sections of the instrument which have become stuck together
7. Recork a key
8. Replace and seat a pad in one of the keys of the upper section and in one of the large keys located on the lower section of the instrument
9. Adjust the bridge mechanism for the auxiliary fingering of B♭ and E♭
10. Replace the fish skin silencers on the two left-hand lever keys of the lower joint (B-E, C♯-F♯)
11. Clean out the register key speaker tube

C. Demonstrate the correct methods and procedures for the following operations.

1. Assemble and disassemble the clarinet
2. Test the instrument for leaks
3. Clean a mouthpiece
4. Swab out the instrument
5. Oil the bore
6. Oil the key mechanism
7. Clean a sticky pad

D. General.

Be able to give instructions on the daily care and maintenance of the clarinets with emphasis on eliminating the common errors or bad habits which lead to the need for repair work.

Chapter 7

OBOE

PLATE XI—OBOE

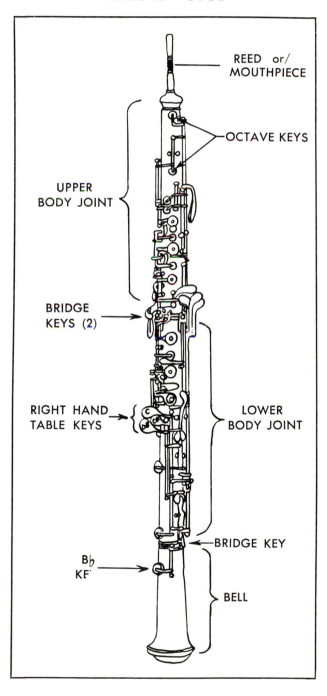

REED or/ MOUTHPIECE

OCTAVE KEYS

UPPER BODY JOINT

BRIDGE KEYS (2)

RIGHT HAND TABLE KEYS

LOWER BODY JOINT

BRIDGE KEY

Bb KF'

BELL

I. ASSEMBLING

The key system of the oboe is not only the most intricate of all the woodwinds, but also the most delicate. A slightly bent key, spring, or missing cork almost always spells disaster.

Because of carelessness, the most frequent damage and repair center around the bridge keys. There are three bridge keys on the oboe; two join the key mechanisms of the upper and lower joint, and the third joins the lower mechanism to the bell. The principle used in joining the three sections is the same as that used with the clarinet; that is, the upper joint must be grasped so as to raise the two bridge keys, and the lower joint must be grasped so that the bridge keys on this section remain down. This means that on the lower section the hand must grasp the instrument below the three table keys C, C♯, and D♯ (see Plate XI). In this manner the two sections can be joined by allowing the upper set of bridge keys to overlap the set on the bottom joint. The bell is joined to the lower section by grasping it so that the thumb presses down on the B♭ key, thus raising the bell bridge key and allowing it to slip over the connecting bridge key from the lower joint.

NOTE: This same procedure, with the exception of adding the bocal to the completely assembled instrument, is followed when assembling the English horn.

II. REPAIRS AND MAINTENANCE

A. Testing and Adjusting for Leaks

The key system of the clarinet is quite elementary compared with that of the oboe. On the clarinet all but a few of the keys work as separate units; whereas on the oboe almost all the keys are part of a system governed by set screws, adjustment screws, levers, and counterbalanced springs.

If an oboe blows "stuffy" and/or fails to respond correctly in rapid passages, the trouble usually can be traced to a leaking pad. Frequently it is a problem of adjustment rather than a bent key or a faulty pad.

Assuming that all keys (pads) are seating well independently, the following is a process for checking the basic mechanism of the oboe.

Adjustment Procedure (with Plate No. XII)

Materials needed:
1. Feeler gauge
2. Small screwdriver
3. Duckbilled or smooth-jawed pliers

Figure 7.1

Figure 7.2

Procedure:

1. Grasping the oboe with the left hand, press R^1 down with the thumb.

   a. With the index finger of the same hand, depress L^2. Notice that L^a is lowered with this action.

   b. Insert the feeler gauge under L^a, depress L^2 and withdraw the gauge—an even drag should result. If not, the key (L^a) is not seating. Locate the small adjustment screw that controls this key and give it about a quarter (clockwise) turn. Continue testing with the feeler gauge until a noticeable drag is produced.

   c. With the feeler gauge, check now to see that L^2 is seating firmly. If not, the adjustment screw for L^a has been turned too far and must be backed off slightly.

   d. Continue checking until both keys seat firmly and evenly as a unit.

2. Repeat this entire procedure with L^3 and L^b.

3. A check must now be made that both L^a and L^b seat well as a unit when R^1 is released.

   a. Insert the feeler gauge under first L^a then L^b and withdraw it as R^1 is pressed and released.

   b. If there is lack of drag on the gauge at this point the adjustment can usually be made with the bridge key (that key which connects the lower section of keys to the upper section). If there is no adjustment screw, the bridge key lever which extends over the joint will have to be bent (up or down) to correct the problem.

4. Depress and hold down L^4 (G♯/A♭).

   a. Place the feeler gauge under the pad that comes up when L^4 is depressed (G♯/A♭).

   b. Depress R^1—this should in turn also depress the raised key (G♯/A♭).

   c. Withdraw the feeler gauge and check for a drag.

   d. If little or no drag is evident, either correct with the small adjustment screw or bend the key bar that is involved up or down.

   e. Check with the gauge to make certain too much adjustment has not been made and that both the (G♯/A♭) key and R^1 seat respectively.

5. Using the left-hand thumb again, depress the R^2 key with the thumb.

PLATE XII—OBOE ADJUSTMENT DIAGRAM

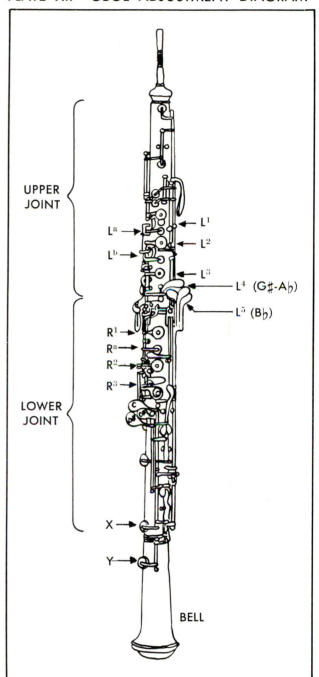

   a. Insert the feeler gauge under R^a, release R^2, and check for a drag. If none, locate the small adjustment screw between these two keys and correct as instructed previously.

   b. Insert the gauge under R^2, depress, and check for a drag. If none, the adjustment screw that regulates R^2 and R^a has been turned too far and must be backed off slightly. Both keys (R² and Rᵃ) must seat together.

6. Some oboes have an F resonator key located near and connected to R³. Place the feeler gauge under this resonator key, depress R³, and check the seating situation of this key. Again, if no drag or a very light drag is noticed, it must be corrected. Locate the small adjustment key that controls this key; regulate and recheck until an even drag results between the resonator key and R³.

7. Depress L⁵ (low B♭ key). This in turn depresses two padded keys (X and Y) over their respective tone holes.

   a. Repeat this action while using the feeler gauge first under one and then the other (X and Y). Determine if either of the two keys is not seating properly.

   b. The adjustment for this is made by bending (up or down) the bridge key that connects the key mechanisms of the lower joint to the B♭ key on the bell.

These steps should eliminate many of the common problems associated with the instrument's proper playing ability. It must be realized that with the many different styles, makes, and models, other adjustments occur, and some mentioned above are redundant and should be ignored.

If all the checking possibilities have been made, and all obvious reasons as broken keys and springs have been eliminated, and the tone production of all or some tones is still not acceptable, the instrument, because of its delicate structure and sensitive mechanism, should be taken to a competent repairman.

B. Octave Key Speaker Tubes

Located on the upper part of the body of the oboe are two octave keys (see Plate XI). Under each key is a very small speaker tube which must be kept clean. If either or both of these holes is obstructed by dirt, lint, or even saliva, the production of several high tones of the instrument, especially high G, A, and B, are seriously hampered.

Saliva in a speaker tube creates a fear common to all oboe players. Although its presence cannot be eliminated, the problem it creates can be handled and, if necessary, reduced to a minimum.

If the problem occurs only occasionally it is simply a matter of removing the water. For this it is wise to keep a package of cigarette paper on hand. The process for removing the water is as follows.

Procedure:

1. Remove the reed.
2. Remove the upper body joint from the lower body joint.
3. Place a piece of cigarette paper under one of the octave keys.
4. With the left hand, cover all tone holes on the body. With the right hand, close off the hole at the end of the joint.
5. Blow hard into the upper, open end and at the same time raise the octave key, which the paper is under, up and down several times. The water will be forced out of the tube and become absorbed by the paper.
6. Remove the wet paper, shift it to a dry spot and repeat the process until the paper comes out dry.
7. Repeat the entire operation with the other octave key.

If this problem recurs constantly, the instrument should be taken to a competent repairman who can perform a more permanent remedy. This operation requires taking both of the speaker tubes out and coating the little "wells" which face the inside bore of the instrument with petroleum jelly. It should be made certain that no petroleum jelly gets into the hole of the speaker tube.

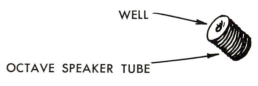

WELL

OCTAVE SPEAKER TUBE

Figure 7.3

The reason for this operation is that when the "well" is dry it attracts saliva like a blotter; when the "well" is coated with petroleum jelly it repels the saliva and allows it to run over or around the area of the hole in the speaker tube.

Moisture is not the sole reason for a speaker tube's clogging up. Sometimes pieces of dirt, lint, and even tobacco are blown up into the holes. The process of cleaning them out should not be put off until the necessity arises, but should be done periodically, the same as the oiling of the bore or key mechanism.

A small feather, broomstraw, or thin sliver of wood is used to clean out the tubes after the octave keys have been removed. A pin or any metal object never should be used. The bores of the speaker tubes are very sensitive, and if they are scratched or enlarged the intonation of the instrument will suffer.

III. SPECIAL TIPS

A. Swabbing

Because of the small bore of the oboe, too much emphasis cannot be put on the practice of habitually swabbing out the instrument after every use. The process is of a dual nature. The swab removes moisture and saliva as well as dust collected and held by the bore oil and any other foreign matter which has been blown into the instrument. The swab usually used in the oboe is a turkey or pheasant feather. To be most effective, the feather should be as straight as possible. To straighten a turkey or pheasant feather, bend it slightly in the opposite direction and in this position pin it to a board. The feather is then steamed and allowed to dry. Another very successful type of swab is made by tying a small piece of silk cloth to a weighted cord. The weight is dropped through the bore from the large end and the cloth pulled through after it. Care should be taken not to use a large piece of cloth at first or it may become lodged in the small tapered end.

Some swabs are made of nylon or mohair; some are made of cotton, similar to a pipe cleaner. These do an excellent job of cleaning out the inside, but often leave small lint deposits in the bore. This lint can cause considerable trouble if blown into a small tone hole.

B. Oiling the Bore

To minimize cracking, the bore of the oboe should be oiled very liberally about twice a year depending on the amount of use, the age of the instrument, and the climate. In the process of oiling, all pads which are normally closed should have a piece of paper or blotter inserted between the pad and the tone hole. This will prevent the pad from soaking up oil from the swab or from the body of the instrument itself. One effective means of oiling the bore is to hold the section to be oiled up at a slightly slanted angle, making sure that a section of the body which does not have any tone holes is facing downward. A small amount of bore oil is then run into the bore and allowed to run down the entire length of the section. The feather or swab is then inserted and twirled to spread the oil evenly over the inside of the bore.

C. The Reed

The reed of the oboe also must be cleaned periodically. This is done by running lukewarm water through it. A small feather may be used to clean it further. Almost all commercial reeds, when purchased, are in a small plastic or glass vial. If this vial is used to store the reed in after it has been played, the reed must be thoroughly dried out before it is put away. If this is impossible, the cap should be left off the tube so the reed can dry properly or holes can be drilled into the plastic tube at numerous places for ventilation. Never put a wet reed away in a sealed container! The best reed case is one which allows proper ventilation.

D. Loose Posts

Mention has been made earlier in the text regarding the cause and remedy of loose posts. On the oboe, due to strong springs and/or the angle of pressure, there are two areas of special concern.

The first is the top post which holds the low C key near the key spatula. The second is the bottom post of the second (side) octave key spatula. If problems occur when producing tones involving these keys, check the key posts and their pivot screws.

IV. INSTRUMENT INSPECTION CHECK SHEET

Oboe and English Horn

Instrument. . . . .   Serial Number.   Make. . . . .

School. . . . .   Private. . . . .   School or Manufacturer's Number . . . .

Finish. . . . .   Other Notations . . . .

		Needs	
O.K.		Attention	

BODY

.... 1. Are there any signs of cracking?

....2. Are there any chipped tone holes?

.... 3. Do any of the tone holes need cleaning?

.... 4. Are any of the tenons broken or badly chipped?

.... 5. Is the thumb rest loose?

.... 6. Are there any loose tenon or bell rings?

.... 7. Are the tenons well corked so that there is no play when the sections are fitted together?

.... 8. Does the wood look dried out and in need of oil?

.... 9. Are there tenon caps or protectors for the corked joints?

....10. (Other comments)

KEY MECHANISM

....1. Are there any bent or broken keys (check especially the bridge keys)?

....2. Are there any pivot screws or key rods missing?

....3. Do all keys operate freely and easily?

....4. Are the corks missing from any of the keys?

....5. Is the key system overly noisy (due to missing corks or lack of oil)?

....6.

PADS

....1. Are there any loose or missing pads?

.... 2. Are there any pads in bad condition (torn, hard or brittle, seating improperly, sticking)?

....3.

CASE

....1. Does the case need repair (hinges, locks, or handle)?

....2. Does the instrument fit securely in the case?

....3. Are there any accessories lying loose in the case which can damage the instrument?

....4.

ENGLISH HORN

....1. Are any of the bocals bent or damaged?

....2. Do any of the bocals need recorking?

....3.

OTHER COMMENTS

Date . . . .

(signature)

V. CLASS PROJECT SHEET*

Oboe and English Horn

A. Know the names of the various parts of the instrument.

B. Be able to perform the following operations using the correct procedures, techniques, and tools.

   1. Reset a loose post using:

      a. emery powder or grit from a piece of sandpaper
      b. dental floss
      c. emery washer

   2. Remove a needle spring and replace it with a new one
   3. Perform emergency measures to remedy a loose tenon using:

      a. cork grease and heat
      b. dental floss

   4. Recork a key
   5. Replace and seat one of the bladder-type pads
   6. Clean out the speaker tube located under each of the two octave keys

C. Demonstrate the correct methods and procedures for the following operations.

   1. Assemble and disassemble the oboe and English horn
   2. Test the instrument for leaks
   3. Clean an oboe or English horn reed
   4. Swab out the instrument
   5. Oil the bore
   6. Oil the key mechanism
   7. Clean a sticky pad

D. General.

Be able to give instructions on the daily care and maintenance of the oboe and English horn, with emphasis on eliminating the common errors or bad habits which lead to the need for repair work.

*It may be that several of these operations can be bypassed because they have been covered in the project sheet of the preceding chapter.

Chapter 8

BASSOON

PLATE XIII—BASSOON

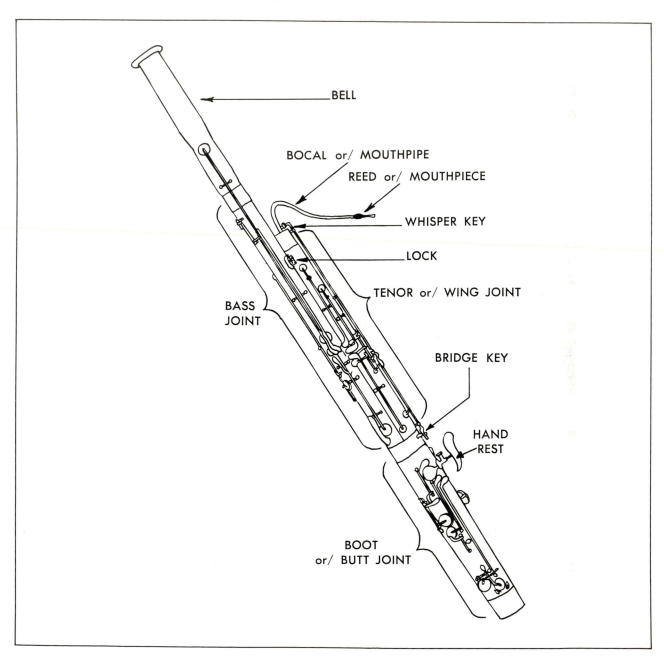

BELL

BOCAL or/ MOUTHPIPE

REED or/ MOUTHPIECE

WHISPER KEY

LOCK

TENOR or/ WING JOINT

BASS JOINT

BRIDGE KEY

HAND REST

BOOT or/ BUTT JOINT

I. ASSEMBLING

The bassoon is made up of six parts, namely the reed or mouthpiece, the bocal or mouthpipe, the tenor or wing joint, the boot or butt joint, the bass joint, and the bell.

The tenons of the bassoon are very fragile and very costly to replace. To assure that no undue strain or stress is placed upon them the first procedure in assembling the instrument is, therefore, to make certain that all tenons are well greased with either cork grease or mutton tallow.

When this is accomplished, take the boot or butt joint in the right hand holding it so that the hand rest receiver (see Plate XIII) is on the far side of the joint away from the individual. With the left hand grasp the small tenor or wing joint and insert it into the proper socket in the boot using short rotating, twisting motions.

Next, take the large bass joint and, by holding it at the top, insert it into the boot next to the tenor joint (see Fig. 8.2).

If the instrument has a lock assemblage for these two joints, it can now be engaged.

The bell is next put on top of the bass joint. The key on the bell should overlap the rod extending upward on the bass joint.

The bocal, or mouthpipe, is now ready to be added. It should be grasped just above the cork and worked down into the tenor joint. The pipe should never be grasped by the extended portion. It is also necessary that the small pad on the "whisper key" cover the small hole in the bocal.

The last to be assembled is the reed or mouthpiece. When disassembling the instrument the preceding steps should be reversed.

II. REPAIRS AND MAINTENANCE

A. Loose Tenon Rings

As a wooden instrument dries out, the wood shrinks. This process will cause a tenon ring or boot cap to become loose to the extent that either or both of them may drop off completely. The tenon ring is a metal band which fits around the rim of the tenon receiver to reinforce that part of the body. The only one to be concerned with on the bassoon is the ring located on the bell section. The other rings are secured as part of the key mechanism. The boot cap is at the bottom of the boot and covers the

tube which connects the bores of the tenor and bass joints.

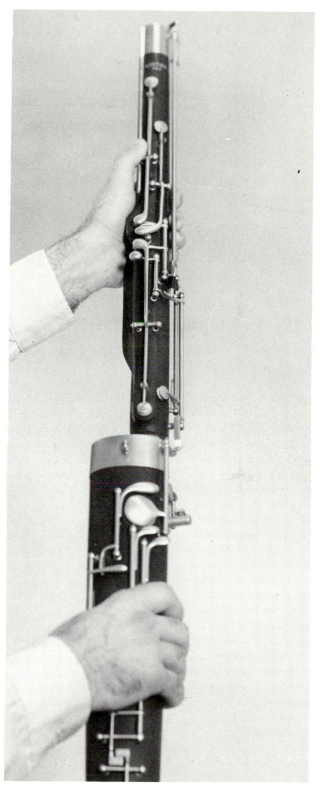

Figure 8.1

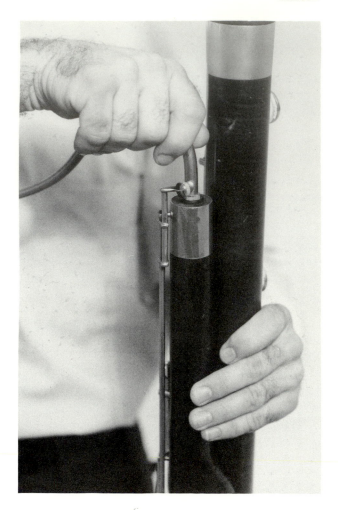

Figure 8.3

If either of these becomes loose, it can be replaced by using a cloth shim. The procedure is as follows.

Materials needed:
1. Strip of cheesecloth or thin linen about eight inches square
2. Razor blade
3. Small rubber, plastic, or rawhide mallet
4. Tube of liquid pad cement (to be used for the tenon ring only)

Procedure: (To refit the bell tenon ring)
1. Remove the loose ring and clean the surfaces of any foreign matter or old glue.
2. Spread a thin coat of pad cement on the ring groove (the area on the bell from which the ring was taken).
3. Stretch the cloth over the end of the tenon.

Figure 8.2

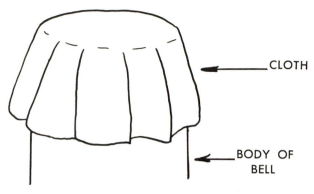

Figure 8.4

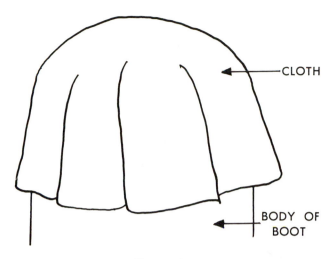

Figure 8.6

4. Replace the ring on the tenon and tap it down. DO NOT tap it all the way on, but leave about 1/32″ clearance. This allows room to cut the surplus cloth away without leaving any loose fringes.

5. Take the razor blade and cut away the surplus cloth from around the bottom of the ring.

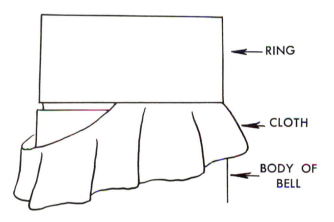

Figure 8.5

6. Next tap the ring all the way on and cut away the cloth that covers the hole at the end.

Procedure: (To refit the boot cap)
1. Remove the cap and clean the surfaces of any foreign matter.
2. DO NOT USE GLUE with the shim on the boot cap!
3. Stretch the cloth over the tube of the boot joint.
4. Replace the cap over the cloth and tap it down. DO NOT tap it all the way on but leave about 1/32″ clearance. This will allow

room to cut the surplus cloth away without leaving any loose fringes.
5. Take the razor blade and cut away the surplus cloth from around the edge of the cap.
6. Tap the cap all the way on.

B. Loose Joints

Most bassoons now have corked tenons, but some still have tenons wound with linen thread coated with beeswax or, as a suitable substitute, dental floss. The beauty of the latter is that when a joint becomes loose, it is a simple matter to wind on a few more strands of thread until a tight fit is obtained. The use of dental floss is a wonderful emergency measure. It can be wound even over a cork tenon which has become loose or used to replace the original cork on a tenon. Another technique which can be used with a corked tenon is to coat the cork with cork grease and rotate it over a flame. The combination of heat plus cork grease will cause the cork to swell and form a temporary, tight-fitting joint. Extreme caution should be observed, however, with the bassoon because of the varnished maple wood which is easily ignited.

C. Recorking the Bocal

Materials needed:
1. Sheet of cork, 1/16″ thick
2. Stick of shellac or contact cement
3. Alcohol burner
4. Several feet of string
5. Razor blade

Procedure:

1. Scrape all cork and cement from the area to be corked.
2. Measure the width needed to cover the area, estimate the length needed to encircle the tenon (leave ample amount for the bevel), and cut the piece from the sheet of cork.

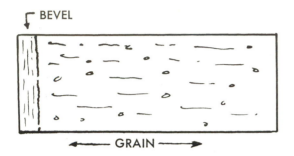

Figure 8.7

3. With the rawhide mallet, pound the cork to break up the stiff fibers and make it pliable.
4. Expose the area to be corked on the bocal to the flame of the alcohol burner. As the metal heats, rotate the tube and apply liberal amounts of melted shellac. Coat the entire area well.

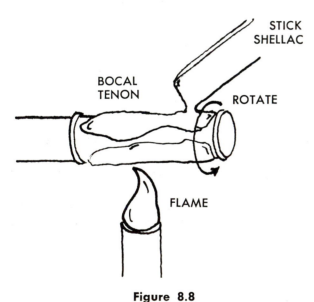

Figure 8.8

5. Quickly remove the bocal from the flame and, while the shellac is still soft, wrap the cork around the tenon pressing it securely and firmly in place.

6. With a heated spatula or heel of a teaspoon apply some melted shellac to the beveled area and press the overlapping section in place.

Figure 8.9

7. Wrap the entire corked tenon with string.
8. Using a soda straw or similar small tube, preferably one that will not burn, blow a small thin stream of fire into the open corked end of the bocal. This will remelt the shellac allowing it to more thoroughly cover the area and penetrate into the cork.

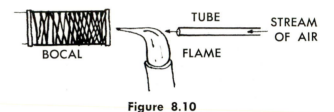

Figure 8.10

9. When the bocal is cool remove the string and cut away the excess amount of cork from the overlapping. Also trim off any shellac that has oozed from under the sides of the cork.
10. Sand for a proper fit.

NOTE: Tenons are also replaced by winding several layers of flax thread coated with beeswax around the area. As the section becomes loose, more thread can be added to eliminate any play.

D. Boot Gasket Leaks

Between the body of the boot joint and the metal tube which connects the tenor bore to the bass bore, is a gasket. This is almost always made of cork and will, on occasion, crack or break causing a leak.

When the boot joint is tested with smoke, the cap should be removed to see if any smoke escapes from around the cork gasket. If it does a new gasket is needed. A temporary measure can be taken, however, until time allows for a new gasket to be refit by a skilled repairman.

Material needed:

Cork grease

Procedure:

1. Unscrew and remove completely both of the screws which hold the tube plate on.

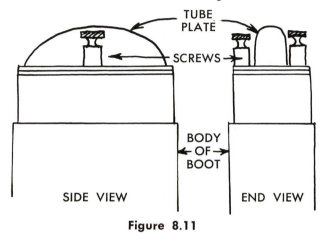

Figure 8.11

2. Remove the tube plate. This must be replaced exactly as it was removed.
3. Coat the top of the cork gasket liberally and evenly with a layer of cork grease.
4. Replace the tube plate.
5. Replace the screws and tighten the plate down. Substances similar to cork grease, other than glue, can be used.

E. Pad Leaks

The pads on a bassoon are made of soft leather and, like any leather exposed to water, varying temperatures, and saliva acids, these pads dry out, become hard and brittle, and eventually crack. If a pad is hard or cracked, it will not seat properly. The following steps can be taken to check for leaks and reseat or replace a bad pad.

If an instrument blows "stuffy" and/or fails to respond in rapid passages, a leaking pad is almost always the cause. Pad leaks usually can be traced to one of two things: either the pad is not seated properly or the skin has become old and broken or torn by abuse or an accident.

To locate the exact pad or pads that are leaking, one joint at a time is tested by the following process.

Procedure:

1. Cover all the holes with the fingers and/or by depressing the keys.

2. Seal one end of the section with either a cork or the palm of the hand.
3. When this is done it is best to stand in front of a mirror so that all keys can be viewed.
4. Blow smoke into the open end.
5. Locate the leak by observing where the smoke seeps out.
6. Examine the pad and determine whether it must be replaced or simply reseated.

F. Reseating a Pad

If the pad is in good condition, but leaking, and in a position where it is possible to expose the backside of the cup to a flame without removing or endangering other keys or pads, the cup should be heated only enough to melt the cement inside.

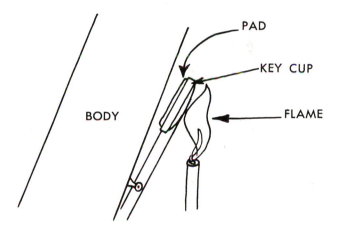

Figure 8.12

The key cup and pad are then pressed back against the tone hole. This will force the pad to shift itself. The cup will be hot, therefore some object should be used to press the key down.

After this operation the pad should again be tested with smoke or a feeler gauge. If the key still leaks, the pad is probably old and hard and should be replaced.

G. Replacing a Pad

Materials needed:

1. Assortment of bassoon, bass clarinet, or saxophone pads
2. Tube of liquid cement
3. Screwdriver

Procedure:

1. It is not necessary to remove the key from the instrument, but it is advisable because it allows a thorough cleaning of the pad cup.
2. After the cup is thoroughly cleaned out, select a new pad that will fit the cup tightly. With a small selection of pads to choose from it may be necessary to use a pad which is smaller than the cup. In an emergency this is permissible; the only criteria is that the pad be large enough to cover the tone hole.
3. Place a liberal amount of liquid cement in the cup and fit the pad in.
4. Replace the key on the instrument, tie the cup and pad down and let it stand for an hour or so until the cement dries. In an emergency it is possible, if the pad fits tightly in the cup, to use the instrument immediately.

III. SPECIAL TIPS

A. Swabbing

Every bassoon should come equipped with a special set of swabs to clean the bass, boot, and tenor joints. However, most of these are made of mohair which has a tendency to leave small deposits of loose lint or fuzz in the bore of the instrument. To prevent this, keep on hand a swatch of old linen or "T-shirt" large enough to completely cover the swab.

Additional care can be given the boot by making a swab similar to a clarinet swab; that is, a piece of cloth six to eight inches square with a weighted cord, long enough to reach through the entire bore of the boot joint, tied to one corner. After the water is dumped out of the boot the swab is pulled through it to remove the remainder of the moisture.

The bocal is the section of the instrument which usually receives the least amount of cleaning care. One procedure is to run warm water through the tube. This, however, should only precede a good swabbing, not replace it. A swab can be made by joining together several pipe cleaners or by using a "test tube brush" which may be a little difficult to acquire, but is well worth any efforts to do so.[1] The small breather hole in the side of the tube should also be cleaned periodically. This is best done with a broomstraw or a thin sliver of wood. No metal pins or wires should ever be used. The size of the hole is very important to the correct blowing of the instrument, and it may become enlarged if a metal cleaning tool is used.

In the cleaning process the reed must not be forgotten. It should be rinsed in warm water and a feather run through it to remove any foreign matter or saliva acids that have collected inside.

B. Sticky Pads

The pads also may be cleaned if they become sticky. Some musicians sprinkle a small amount of talcum powder on a piece of paper, place this between the pad and the tone hole and depress the key. The powder immediately absorbs the moisture and covers the sticky area with a dry coating. As can be understood, this is a very temporary and not too efficient method of eliminating a common problem. A more lasting and efficient procedure is to dampen one end of a pipe cleaner with denatured alcohol and wipe the pad clean with this. The dry end of the cleaner is used to remove any excess alcohol on the pad immediately. After this has been done, another pipe cleaner with a small amount of key oil on one end is run lightly over the pad. This latter step is essential because the alcohol will dry out the skin of the pad and cause it to crack if some of the oil is not replaced.

C. Oiling

As has been mentioned, the body or bore of the bassoon is not oiled. The moving metal parts, however, should be oiled about twice a year. This is done by dipping a pin or toothpick in a fine grade of key oil and applying it to all points of friction such as pivot screws, rods, and even the springs. This will prevent rusting, minimize wear, and assure efficient key action.

The tone holes should be kept clean. "Q-Tips" or a small wad of cotton on a toothpick or match works nicely for this operation.

As an ounce of prevention, it is prudent to coat the exposed edges of the tone holes with bore oil or olive oil to prevent any drying-out process.

1. An excellent bocal brush can be obtained from John Grant, 3729 N. Oketo Ave., Chicago, Ill. 60634.

IV. INSTRUMENT INSPECTION CHECK SHEET

Bassoon

Instrument. . . . . Serial Number. . . . . Make. . . . .

School. . . . . Private. . . . . School or Manufacturer's Number . . . .

Finish. . . . . Other Notations . . . .

| | Needs | |
| O.K. | Attention | |

BOCAL

. . . .	. . . .	1. Is the bocal bent or dented?
. . . .	. . . .	2. Is there anything in the bore to constrict the proper flow of air (blow through it)?
. . . .	. . . .	3. Is the whisper key hole clogged (blow through it)?
. . . .	. . . .	4. Is the tenon properly wound or corked?
. . . .	. . . .	5. (Other comments)

BODY

1. Are any of the tenons chipped or broken?
2. Are all the tenons properly wound or corked to fit firmly and securely together with no play?
3. Are there any loose tenon or bell rings?
4. Is the lock mechanism (holds tenor and bass joints together) broken or loose?
5. Is the hand rest receiver broken or loose?
6. Is the boot cap loose?
7. Are there any cracks or chipped tone holes?
8.

KEY MECHANISM

1. Are there any bent or broken keys?
2. Are there any pivot screws or key rods missing?
3. Do all keys work freely and easily?
4. Is the key system overly noisy (due to missing corks or lack of oil)?
5.

PADS

1. Are there any loose or missing pads?
2. Are there any pads in bad condition (torn, hard or brittle, seating improperly, sticking)?
3.

CASE

1. Does the case need repair (hinges, locks, or handle)?
2. Is there a set of swabs for the instrument?
3. Are there any accessories lying loose in the case which can damage the instrument?
4.

OTHER COMMENTS

Date . . . .

(signature)

V. CLASS PROJECT SHEET

Bassoon

A. Know the names of the various parts of the instrument.

B. Be able to perform the following operations using the correct procedures, techniques, and tools.

    1. Perform emergency measures to remedy a loose tenon using:

        a. cork grease and heat
        b. dental floss

    2. Recork a key
    3. Replace a pad
    4. Refit a loose tenon ring and boot cap
    5. Seal a leaking gasket on the boot joint

C. Demonstrate the correct methods and procedures for the following operations.

    1. Assemble and disassemble the bassoon
    2. Clean the bocal including the whisper key tube
    3. Swab out the instrument
    4. Oil the key mechanism
    5. Clean a sticky pad
    6. Clean the reed

D. General.

Be able to give instructions on the daily care and maintenance of the bassoon with emphasis on eliminating the common errors or bad habits which lead to the need for repair work.

Chapter 9

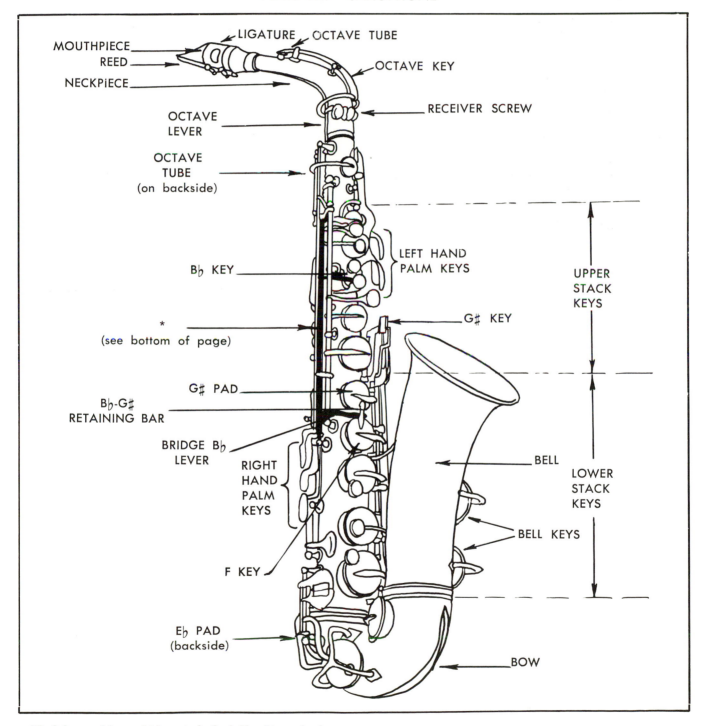

SAXOPHONES

PLATE XIV—SAXOPHONE

MOUTHPIECE

REED

NECKPiECE

LIGATURE   OCTAVE TUBE

OCTAVE KEY

RECEIVER SCREW

OCTAVE LEVER

OCTAVE TUBE (on backside)

Bb KEY

LEFT HAND PALM KEYS

UPPER STACK KEYS

* (see bottom of page)

G♯ KEY

G♯ PAD

Bb-G♯ RETAINING BAR

BRIDGE Bb LEVER

RIGHT HAND PALM KEYS

BELL

LOWER STACK KEYS

BELL KEYS

F KEY

Eb PAD (backside)

BOW

*Rod, key, and lever which controls the bridge Bb mechanism.

I. ASSEMBLING

There is very little difficulty encountered in assembling the saxophone. One precaution should be mentioned, however. This is the process of joining the neckpiece to the body and engaging the octave mechanism properly. There are several types of octave mechanisms, but they are all basically the same; that is, a lever extends upward from the body and engages a ring or bar on the neckpiece. With proper instruction and a little common sense (especially with beginners), many adjustment and repair problems can be eliminated.

The tenon of the neckpiece should be greased with cork grease so there will be no undue strain in assembling it with the body. Once it is in place the receiver screw should be firmly tightened. On some models the screw is part of the neckpiece while on others it is located on the body.

The last piece to assemble is the mouthpiece. It should never be forced on when the cork is dry or if the instrument has been subjected to a cold atmosphere. Cork becomes brittle when cold and will easily chip and crack. The cork tenon should be well coated with cork grease and the mouthpiece put on with short, twisting movements. The grease will soften as well as preserve the cork and allow the mouthpiece to slip on easily.

II. THE KEY MECHANISM

A. Testing for Leaks

If the instrument plays extremely hard or completely fails to blow, the trouble is almost always a bent key and/or a pad with an extremely bad leak. Several procedures can be used to detect the faulty key or pad.

One procedure is to play the instrument starting at the top (B♮ on the third line). If this tone fails to come out the leak is above this, most likely in the left-hand palm keys. If the B♮ sounds, proceed down the instrument until the bad note is reached—this will be the general area in which to look for the faulty pad or bent key. When the search has narrowed down to three or four pads and the cause cannot be found readily, a feeler gauge can be used to test the pads. The tip of the gauge is inserted between the pad and the rim of the tone hole, the key is depressed and the gauge slowly withdrawn. If the pad is seating correctly at this point a noticeable drag will be felt on the gauge. The procedure should be repeated at several points around the pad until the leak is found or it is certain that the pad is not leaking.

Another method is to seal the bell and close the keys over all the tone holes. Smoke is then blown into the mouthpipe and will seep out wherever there is a leak. After the leaky key or keys are located, the feeler gauge is used to find the exact spot of the leak around the pad.

A professional repairman uses a "leak light" to find any leaks. This is a small bulb (similar to a flashlight bulb) on a long electric cord and activated by battery or electricity and a transformer. It is used with saxophones, large clarinets, and bassoons. The light is dropped down the bore of the instrument with the bulb stopped under each key to be inspected. The key, if not already in a closed position, is depressed *lightly*; any pad can be closed completely if enough pressure is exerted. Inspection is then made around the circumference of the pad and the leak(s) located by noting where the light shows through. This technique is not too effective on the smaller woodwind instruments, which use the bladder-type pad, as the light is easily diffused by the thin fish skin and also the small leaks, which occur on the smaller keys, cannot be readily found.

NOTE: A saxophone may pass all these tests yet play terribly "stuffy" on the low tones. This can be caused by numerous factors.

1. If it is an old horn the pads will be quite dry and deep seated. The leak will go unnoticed because it is hidden and very minute, but if there are enough pads in this condition the sum total will cause the low tones to play stuffily. The only cure is to have the instrument completely repadded.
2. If low C♯, B♮, and B♭ (below the staff) fail to sound or come out only with extreme difficulty, a leak any place on the instrument may be the cause. The leaks need not necessarily be in these specific keys.
3. The G♯ key should be observed closely when any of these three low tones are sounded. On many instruments the mechanism is such that when low C♯, B♮, and B♭ are played the tension is released on the G♯ key. If the G♯ is not in perfect adjustment the key will lift slightly, enough to prevent the low tones from sounding.[1]
4. There are even instances where the low tones will not sound because the wave lengths of sound

1. See the section on "Common Adjustment Problems" for the procedure to check and remedy this situation.

vibrations set in the instrument by the mouthpiece are uneven. By simply moving the mouthpiece in or out a small degree, the vibrations will alter and allow the low tones to sound.

5. Some instruments have soldered-on tone holes. If the instrument is old, the saliva acids may have eaten through the solder causing a leak around the base of one of the tone holes. A leak also may result if the horn is dented near the tone hole or given a severe jolt sufficient to break the solder.

B. Pads and Pad Leaks

The pads on a saxophone are made of soft leather and, like any leather exposed to water, varying temperatures, and saliva acids, these pads dry out, become hard and brittle, and eventually crack. If a pad is hard or cracked it will not seat properly.

Once the exact location of the leak has been determined, an inspection of the pad should be made to see if it has been damaged or is so old and hard it must be replaced. If neither of these is the case steps should be taken to seal the leak.

If the leak is in the back of the cup, the blade of a table knife is inserted under the front part of the pad. By tapping on the key bar with a rubber or rawhide mallet the bar will bend and level the cup. The cup itself should never be struck.

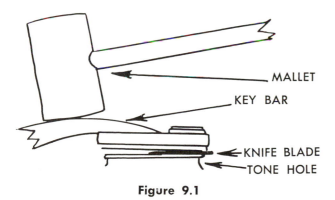

Figure 9.1

If there is not enough room to use the blade of a table knife, a coin such as a fifty-cent piece, or a *saxophone reed* may be substituted.

It is best, if possible, to use hand pressure rather than the mallet to prevent denting the pad cup.

Each time a cup or key rod is bent back into place, the feeler gauge should be used to check to see if the leak has been eliminated. When the pad is seating correctly it can be wet slightly and clamped or tied down for a period of time. This will recrease the pad

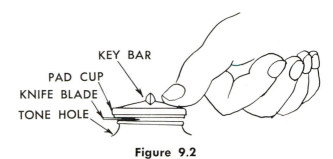

Figure 9.2

and put a new airtight seal between it and the tone hole. If a pad falls out a dab of liquid pad cement can be placed in the cup and the same pad reset. This will not assure an accurate fit but will do until the pad can be replaced.

C. Replacing a Pad

If a pad falls out and is lost or is badly worn and must be replaced, the following steps should be taken.

Materials needed:

1. Assortment of bassoon, bass clarinet, or saxophone pads
2. Tube of liquid cement
3. Screwdriver

Procedure:

1. It is not necessary to remove the key from the instrument, but it is advisable because it allows a thorough cleaning of the pad cup.
2. After the cup is thoroughly cleaned out, select a new pad that will fit the cup tightly. With a small selection of pads to choose from it may be necessary to use a pad which is smaller than the cup. In an emergency this is permissible. The only criteria is that the pad be large enough to cover the tone hole.
3. Place a liberal amount of liquid cement in the cup and fit the pad in.
4. Replace the key on the instrument, tie the cup and pad down and let it stand for an hour or so until the cement dries. (In an emergency it is possible, if the pad fits tightly in the cup, to use the instrument immediately.)
5. Test with a feeler gauge when the cement is dry.

D. Sticky Pads

The bore of the saxophone is very difficult to clean. This is especially true on the larger instruments.

There are swabs that can be run through the instrument after each playing, but they are not particularly efficient as a rule.

Saliva, which is blown into the instrument, is absorbed by any pads with which it comes in contact. This will cause the pads to stick shut and eventually rot. This frequently happens with the G♯ and the E♭ keys, both of which are closed keys and lie in the general path of the saliva flow.

If a pad becomes sticky or is actually stuck shut it should and can be cleaned by swabbing it with a pipe cleaner that has been dipped in carbon tetrachloride, denatured alcohol, or benzine. If denatured alcohol is used, care must be taken not to get it on any lacquered part of the instrument. A second pipe cleaner dipped in oil should be brushed over the pad to replace the natural oil in the leather removed by the alcohol. The rim of the tone hole should be cleaned at the same time. This can be done with a nail file, a knife, or a piece of fine sandpaper.

A quick but very temporary trick used by many professional musicians is to take a dollar bill, place

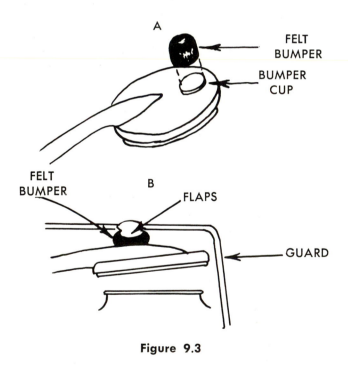

Figure 9.3

it between the pad and the tone hole rim, depress the pad and pull the bill out. Because of the texture of the bill it will absorb some of the foreign matter as well as clean off anything that is on the rim of the tone hole.

E. Bumpers

The bumpers are the small felt pieces most often located on the E♭, low C, and bell keys. They are placed there primarily to regulate the height of the open bell keys. The most common types are either set into a round cup on the key or squeezed between two brass flaps above the key.

To replace type A follow these steps.

Materials needed:
1. Assorted felt bumpers
2. Liquid pad cement
3. Razor blade

Procedure:
1. With a small screwdriver clean the old glue out of the cup.
2. The old bumper should be used to determine the diameter and thickness of the new bumper. If the old bumper has been lost a comparison can be made with other bumpers on the instrument. If this also is impossible, select a bumper that is too thick; it can be cut to size later. The width of the felt should be slightly larger than the cup so that it must be squeezed in. This assures a tight fit.

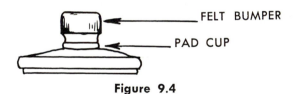

Figure 9.4

3. Place a dab of liquid pad cement in the cup and fit the bumper in; if any cement oozes out wipe off immediately.
4. Determine the height of the bumper by comparing the opening between the pad and the tone hole with the immediate surrounding keys. Adjust the height of the bumper by cutting off the top with the razor blade.

To install type B the same materials are needed, with the exception of the cement. The procedure is as follows.

1. Select a bumper and fit it between the two brass flaps located on the guard directly over the key.
2. Squeeze the flaps together to hold the bumper securely.

BUMPER MUST BE CUT OFF
TO EVEN THE HEIGHT

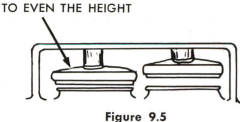

Figure 9.5

3. Adjust the height by cutting off the edge of the felt.

F. Key Recorking

Corks are cemented on the keys for two reasons: to eliminate noise and for adjustment purposes. Regardless of which factor is involved, if a cork breaks off a key the outcome is certain to impair the playing ability of the instrument in some way or other.

There are two methods of replacing a lost or damaged cork on a key. One is to use liquid cement; the other, to use heat and stick shellac. Although the second is quicker, extreme caution and reserve must be observed when working with a lacquered instrument. Lacquered keys can be heated enough to melt stick shellac, but anything beyond that will cause the lacquer to burn. Caution should also be taken when working with keys that have pearl buttons on them—these too burn quite easily. Two methods are outlined.

Materials needed: (Using liquid cement or contact cement)

1. Liquid pad cement or contact cement
2. Pieces of cork 1/16″ thick. This thickness of cork is the one used most extensively on the instrument; if a thinner piece is needed it can be cut down after it is cemented to the key.
3. Razor blade
4. Prick punch

Procedure 1:

1. From the sheet of cork cut a piece as close to the size desired as possible.
2. Stick the prick punch into the edge of the cork then smear a small dab of cement on the cork. If contact cement is used, the key also must be coated. Then observe directions on the container for drying time.

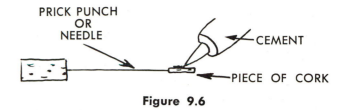
PRICK PUNCH
OR
NEEDLE

CEMENT

PIECE OF CORK

Figure 9.6

3. Work the cork into place, press the key down onto the cork, and withdraw the prick punch. Do not press so hard as to squeeze out the cement.

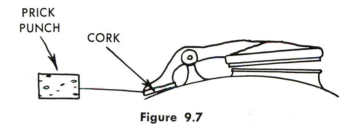
PRICK PUNCH

CORK

Figure 9.7

4. The cement will hold the cork in place; the key need not be held down.
5. The cork can be trimmed if necessary after the cement is thoroughly dry. However, it is best to leave it alone if it is serving its purpose mechanically.

Materials needed: (For heat and stick shellac)

1. Cork (sheets of 1/16″ and 1/64″ are the most common)
2. Razor blade
3. Stick shellac
4. Alcohol burner or cigarette lighter
5. Piece of fine sandpaper
6. Wet cloth
7. Small screwdriver

Procedure 2:

1. Remove the key concerned from the body of the saxophone.
2. With the razor blade, scrape off the old cork and glue.
3. Using the old cork as a pattern, select the correct thickness of cork and cut a piece larger than needed from the sheet. If the old cork is lost, compare the key with one on another saxophone or simply guess.
4. Heat the key, applying the flame to the side opposite that on which the cork is to be ap-

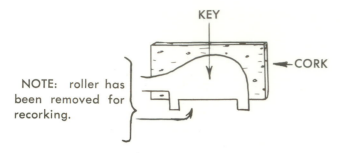

NOTE: roller has been removed for recorking.

Figure 9.8

plied, and at the same time apply the stick shellac to the area to be corked. Smear a thin coat over the required area. Use only enough heat to melt the stick shellac.

5. Remove the key from the flame and press the cork onto the key firmly. Do not press too hard, however, or the shellac will be squeezed out. If a wet cloth is used to set the key on, the shellac will harden more quickly.

Figure 9.9

6. If a wet cloth is used the shellac will be set in about ten seconds. The next procedure is to trim away the excess cork with the razor blade. In doing so, always cut toward the key rather than away from it so as not to tear the cork from the key. Make all cuts slanting, thus leaving neat, beveled edges.

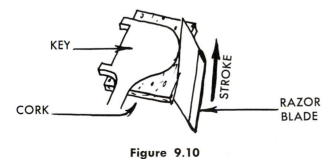

Figure 9.10

7. The last step is to smooth the beveled surfaces with sandpaper.

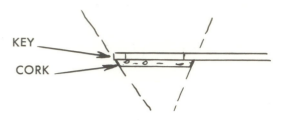

Figure 9.11

8. Check to make sure the new cork allows the key to operate properly. If it is one which regulates the opening of a tone hole, a small amount may have to be sanded or cut off to allow the cup to rise to the proper height (at least 1/4″).

G. Springs

It is not advisable to tamper with the needle springs on a saxophone. This is not because they are more delicate than those on a clarinet, but simply because most of them are located in areas very difficult for the layman to reach without removing a series of keys. If, however, the need arises to replace a needle spring, check first to see which type it is. Some manufacturers use a screw-base type rather than those which are simply wedged in.

Occasionally a spring will become dislodged from its hook on the key. If this happens, the process is to find the key and, using a spring hook, (made by filing a notch in the end of a crochet hook) replace the spring.

The other type of spring on the saxophone is the flat spring. These are located mainly on the left-hand palm keys, the right-hand palm keys, and the octave keys. If one of these breaks, the process is to simply take off the key (fortunately they are quite exposed and easy to remove), unscrew the small screw which holds the spring to the key, match as closely as possible the broken spring to the small assortment on hand, and replace it. Tension can be added to the spring by bending it more; straightening will lessen the tension.

If a spring breaks off, a rubber band is a good substitute, but never a replacement. Rubber contains sulphur which will cause a chemical reaction strong enough to eat into the metal as well as tarnish the entire instrument.

Periodically the springs of the instrument should be oiled to retard rust and corrosion.

III. THE NECKPIECE

A. Recorking

Materials needed:

1. Sheet of cork, 1/16" thick
2. Stick of shellac or contact cement
3. Alcohol burner
4. Several feet of string
5. Razor blade

Procedure:

1. Scrape all cork and cement from the area to be corked.
2. Measure the width needed to cover the area, estimate the length needed to encircle the tenon (leave ample amount for the bevel) and cut the piece from the sheet of cork.

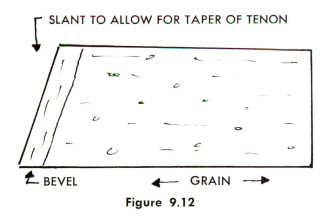

SLANT TO ALLOW FOR TAPER OF TENON

BEVEL   ← GRAIN →

Figure 9.12

3. With the rawhide mallet, pound the cork to break up the stiff fibers and make it pliable.
4. Expose the tenon of the mouthpipe to the flame of the alcohol burner. As the metal heats, rotate the tube and apply liberal amounts of melted shellac. Coat the entire area well.
5. Quickly remove the mouthpipe from the flame and, while the shellac is still soft, wrap the cork around the tenon, pressing it securely and firmly in place.

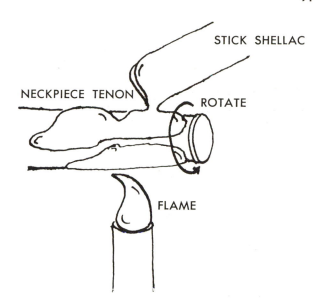

STICK SHELLAC

NECKPIECE TENON

ROTATE

FLAME

Figure 9.13

6. With a heated spatula or heel of a teaspoon, apply some melted shellac to the beveled area and press the overlapping section in place.
7. Wrap the entire corked tenon with string.
8. Using a soda straw or similar small tube, preferably one that will not burn, blow a small thin stream of fire into the open corked end of the mouthpipe. This will remelt the shellac allowing it to more thoroughly cover the area and penetrate into the cork.

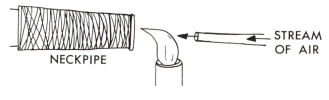

NECKPIPE   STREAM OF AIR

Figure 9.14

9. When the tenon is cool, remove the string and cut away the excess amount of cork from the overlapping. Also trim off any shellac that has oozed from under the sides of the cork.
10. Sand for a proper fit.

B. Care and Emergency Repair

There are two general types of corked tenons onto which the mouthpiece is placed. One (Fig. 9.15) is a tenon tapered so the mouthpiece fits on tightly but can be moved in or out to tune the instrument.

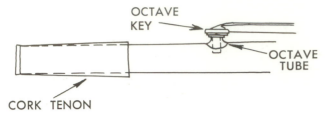

Figure 9.15

The other is a corked tenon less tapered (Fig. 9.16); the mouthpiece fits on and is left in one place. All tuning is done with a tuning ring which is screwed back and forth to lengthen or shorten the neckpiece, thus tuning the instrument.

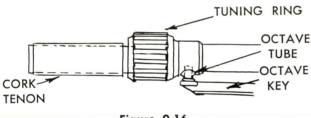

Figure 9.16

The mouthpiece should never be left on the neckpiece when the instrument is put away. This will cause the cork to become permanently compressed, and it eventually will develop into a wobbly, leaky fit. The cork tenon should also be kept well greased. The cork grease helps to preserve the cork as well as assure an easy fit.

If, as eventually will happen to any instrument, the mouthpiece becomes loose on the tenon, temporary adjustments can be made. One is to coat the

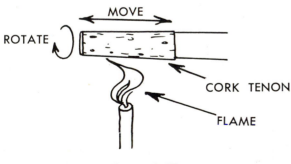

Figure 9.17

tenon well with cork grease and rotate it over a flame. Care must be taken to keep the cork moving so as not to burn it.

This will cause the cork to swell, thus providing a temporary tight fit for the mouthpiece. This can be repeated several times before it loses its effectiveness. Another simpler procedure is to wrap a piece of paper around the tenon and fit the mouthpiece over it.

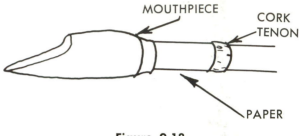

Figure 9.18

Eventually, of course, the tenon must be recorked for which the preceding steps should be followed.

IV. COMMON ADJUSTMENT PROBLEMS

A. Octave Mechanism

There are several types of octave mechanisms on the saxophone, but they are all basically the same; that is, a lever extends upward from the body of the saxophone and engages a ring or bar on the neckpiece.

If the instrument fails to sound any notes in the low register and only those in the high register, the octave mechanism is out of adjustment. This happens quite frequently with the ring type. The ring becomes bent and consequently the octave key on the neckpiece is held open at all times. To remedy

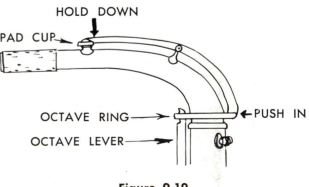

Figure 9.19

this the ring is simply bent back in place while holding the pad cup down.

To check the adjustment A and G above the staff should be played alternately. When G is played the octave key on the neckpiece should be down (closed). When A is played the octave key should be up (open).

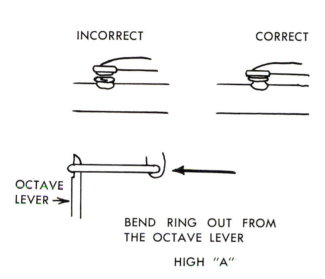

HIGH "G"

INCORRECT   CORRECT

OCTAVE LEVER →

BEND RING OUT FROM
THE OCTAVE LEVER

HIGH "A"

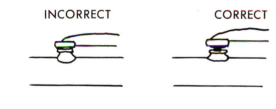

INCORRECT   CORRECT

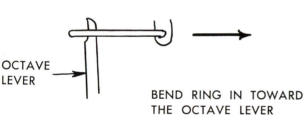

OCTAVE
LEVER

BEND RING IN TOWARD
THE OCTAVE LEVER

Figure 9.20

With the octave key underneath the neckpiece, as on the Conn saxophone, the octave key is likewise open when high A is played and closed when high G is played. To adjust this type simply bend the lower part of the octave key rod to correct any error.

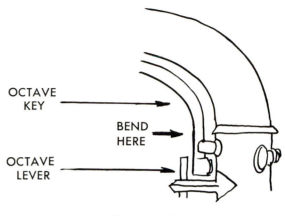

OCTAVE
KEY →

BEND
HERE →

OCTAVE
LEVER →

Figure 9.21

The key is bent away from the body if it does not open when high A is played and toward the body if it does not close when high G is played.

Most saxophones have an end plug which fits into the small end of the body when the neckpiece is removed. This should always be inserted when the instrument is put away to assure proper blocking of the instrument in the case and to protect the octave mechanism.

B. Octave Tubes

One of these little pipes is located on the neckpiece and the other on the top part of the body (see Plate No. XIV). The breather holes in these tubes are very small and if dirt collects in them it can cause a great deal of trouble. They therefore should be cleaned periodically. This can be done by running a feather or pipe cleaner through the hole.

C. Bridge B♭[2]

This mechanism is one which frequently is out of adjustment but, because it seldom is used, it is more often suffered with than repaired. The adjustment is made on a small retaining bar located on the first key of the lower stack. This engages a lever (bridge B♭ lever) which automatically holds down the upper B♭ key (see Plate XIV).

To check the adjustment, the F key is depressed. A feeler gauge is then used to see which of the two keys is not seating—the B♭ key or the F key. If the B♭ key is not seating the bridge B♭ lever is bent up.

2. Refer to Plate XIV for the location of the F key, the bridge B♭ lever and the B♭ key as mentioned in the following paragraph.

If the F key is not seating the bridge B♭ lever is bent down.

D. G♯ Key

The retaining bar which engages the bridge B♭ lever also holds the G♯ key down and makes the trill up to G♯ possible. This bar must be in perfect adjustment because on many instruments when low C♯, B♮, or B♭ is played, all other tension on the G♯ key is released. The adjustment here can be checked by sight or, better yet, with a feeler gauge.

The mechanism can be tested by fingering F on the instrument and then depressing the left-hand G♯ key. If an adjustment is needed the G♯ pad cup will rise slightly, creating a leak that will prevent the three low tones, before mentioned, from sounding. To remedy this the retaining bar must be bent down to correct the adjustment and stop the leak. On some makes of saxophones a small set screw is provided for the adjustment.

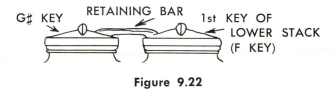

Figure 9.22

V. SPECIAL TIPS

A. Swabbing and Cleaning

All water should be removed from the instrument after each playing. Most of this water collects in the bow end of the body and can be removed by tipping the saxophone up and pouring it out. On the baritone saxophone it collects in the mouthpipe, which is equipped with a water key for removing excess saliva. If the water is not removed, it will drain onto the pads when the instrument is placed in its case and be absorbed by them. The acids in the saliva will dry the pads out and eventually rot them.

Moisture also can be removed from the three left-hand palm keys by holding them open and blowing the water off the pads. If a player tends to blow an excess of water into the instrument, a blotter can be used to dry the pads before putting the instrument away.

The only way to clean out the bore of a saxophone is with a swab made especially for this purpose or a piece of silk or chamois measuring about 12″ × 4″, tied to a piece of fishline long enough to extend from the bell down and around the bow and up through the small opening. A small weight should be attached to the other end of the fishline.

Figure 9.23

The weight should be dropped into the small end, and the saxophone tipped so that the weight falls out the bell end. The swab is then pulled through the bore.

The neckpiece should be cleaned more frequently, using lukewarm water and a flexible brush.

The mouthpiece, it seems, is the section which receives the least attention when it should receive the most. The reed should always be taken off the mouthpiece after each playing, wiped dry, and put in a reed holder or container. The mouthpiece must not be neglected when swabbing out the instrument. The weighted cord should not be used, however, for fear of chipping the tip of the mouthpiece if the weight is carelessly dropped through the chamber. To swab out the mouthpiece use a regular mouthpiece brush or a soft cloth run through the hole. The ligature should be loosened and the reed cap put on to protect the fragile tip of the mouthpiece. Often, due to lack of cleaning, a hard, crusty mold will form inside the chamber of the mouthpiece. No attempt should ever be made to scrape this out with a knife. If the mouthpiece is left to soak in a cup of vinegar overnight, the mold will dissolve and can then be removed with lukewarm water and a brush. A mouthpiece should never be placed in hot water because most of them are made of hard rubber and may warp and/or become discolored.

Caution should be observed at all times when polishing a saxophone to keep the cleaning solution off the pads and out of the key mechanism. If it is necessary to clean under the rods and keys, a soft camel's hair brush or a damp cloth on a stick can be used. Care should be taken not to snag any of the needle springs which are easily bent or broken.

VI. INSTRUMENT INSPECTION CHECK SHEET

Saxophones

Instrument............................. Serial Number..................... Make.............

School........... Private........... School or Manufacturer's Number ....

Finish......................... Other Notations ....

	Needs	
O.K.	Attention	

MOUTHPIECE

1. Does the mouthpiece have a reed cap?
2. Is the tip of the mouthpiece chipped?
3. Does the mouthpiece need cleaning?
4. Is the ligature in good condition (any screws missing)?
5. (Other comments)

BODY

1. Is the neck properly corked (try fitting the mouthpiece on; it should not go on more than two-thirds the way)?
2. Does the neck fit firmly and securely into the body without any play?
3. Are there any large dents in the body, especially near the tone holes?
4. Are there any loose or broken braces, guards, or posts?
5. If the instrument is designed to use an end plug, is it being used?
6.

KEY MECHANISM

1. Are there any bent or broken keys?
2. Are there any pivot screws or key rods missing?
3. Do all keys operate freely and easily?
4. Are there any felt bumpers missing?
5. Are any of the pearl insets on the keys missing?
6. Is the key system overly noisy (missing corks, needs oiling, etc.)?
7.

PADS

1. Are there any loose or missing pads?
2. Are there any pads in bad condition (torn, hard or brittle, seating improperly, sticking, etc.)?
3.

CASE

1. Does the case need repair (hinge, locks, or handle)?
2. Does the instrument fit securely in the case?
3. Are there any accessories lying loose in the case which can damage the instrument?
4.

OTHER COMMENTS

Date ....
                                                          (signature)

VII. CLASS PROJECT SHEET

Saxophones

A. Know the names of the various parts of the instrument.

B. Be able to perform the following operations using the correct procedures, techniques, and tools.

1. Seat a pad by:

   a. bending the pad cup or key bar
   b. reheating the cement in the pad cup and shifting the pad

2. Replace and seat a new pad
3. Replace a felt bumper located:

   a. on the pad cup
   b. on the guard over the key

4. Recork a key using:

   a. liquid cement
   b. heat and stick shellac

5. Replace a flat spring on one of the left-hand palm keys
6. Adjust the octave mechanism
7. Clean the octave key tube on the neckpiece
8. Adjust the bridge B♭ mechanism

C. Demonstrate the correct methods and procedures for the following operations.

1. Assemble and disassemble the saxophone
2. Test the instrument for leaks
3. Clean a mouthpiece
4. Swab out the instrument
5. Oil the key mechanism
6. Clean the body of the instrument, giving the correct attention to a silver or lacquered finish
7. Clean a sticky pad

D. General.

Be able to give instructions on the daily care and maintenance of the saxophones with emphasis on eliminating the common errors or bad habits which lead to the need for repair work.

Chapter 10

FLUTE

PLATE XV—THE FLUTE

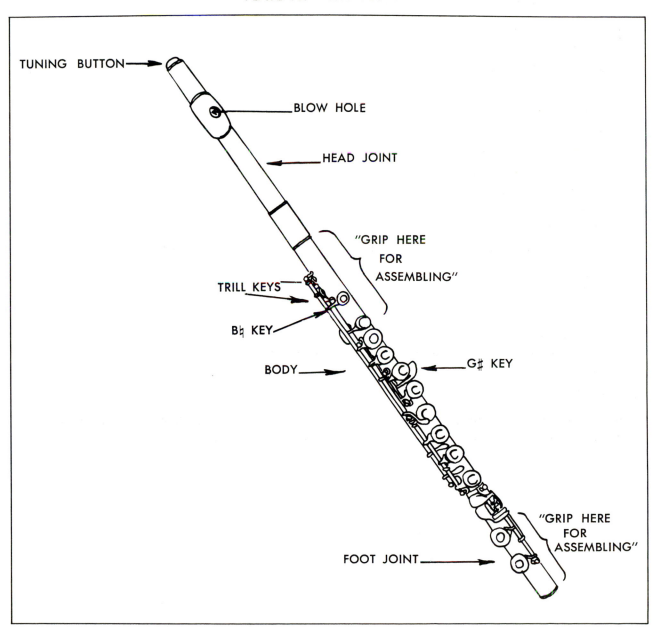

TUNING BUTTON

BLOW HOLE

HEAD JOINT

"GRIP HERE FOR ASSEMBLING"

TRILL KEYS

B♮ KEY

G♯ KEY

BODY

"GRIP HERE FOR ASSEMBLING"

FOOT JOINT

I. ASSEMBLING

Almost all flutes are made in three sections—head joint, body or middle section, and foot joint. The tenon and tuning sleeve on the head joint and tenon on the middle section are seldom greased. If the tenons have not been dented or bent they will work freely without any form of lubrication. To prevent any such mishaps, the tenon caps should be kept on whenever the instrument is put away. If there is trouble in getting the sections together without undue pressure and strain, a little paraffin, tallow, or cork grease can be rubbed on the tenons to reduce friction. If the joints of the instrument become loose and ill-fitting, they can be tightened by "swedging," which can be done at any repair shop.

To assemble the flute, the head joint is first inserted into the middle section and the blow hole set in a straight line with the keys. In assembling the foot joint the instrument should be gripped at the upper end of the middle section and at the bottom end of the foot joint (see Plate XV). The two pieces are then joined with short, twisting movements. The rods and posts of the foot joint should also be in a straight line with the keys of the middle section.

The piccolo, having only two sections (head joint and body), presents no assembly problem.

II. THE KEY MECHANISM

A. Testing for Leaks

The mechanism on the flute, like that on the oboe, is an intricate maze of levers, springs, and adjustment screws, and a leak often is the result of the instrument's being out of adjustment.

Difficulty in playing the low tones of the flute, except for beginners, is one sure sign of a leaking pad. To further test the instrument for pad leaks, each section should be checked separately.

The middle section or body of the flute can be dealt with first.

1. Close one end of the section with a cork or have someone hold his hand over the end to close it off.
2. Close all open holes by depressing the required keys. Use only normal playing pressure.
3. Blow smoke into the open end.
4. Observe where the smoke seeps out. This will indicate a leaking pad.

Repeat the same procedure with the foot joint.

If the pad in question is in good condition but still leaks, the adjustment which controls the key should be checked. This can be done by holding down the pad itself, or having it held down by someone else, instead of using the mechanism which controls it. If this stops the leak the damage is in the adjustment system, which should not be tampered with by anyone not familiar with the mechanism of the instrument.

Most flutes today still use bladder-type pads (fish skin over felt). However, plastic pads are being used with some degree of success. With bladder-type pads, leaks often occur if the fish skin becomes broken or the pad becomes old and the skin hard, dry, and brittle and thus difficult to seat properly. A pad in this condition should be replaced as soon as possible. In an emergency the pad can be reseated to prolong its life. This is done by dampening the pad with a pipe cleaner, tying or clamping it down, and letting it dry. This, in most instances, will temporarily provide an adequate seat and seal any minor leaks.

B. Pad Replacing

If a pad must be replaced it should not be attempted unless the individual knows the instrument well, has the proper tools, and is blessed with a certain degree of mechanical ability. If these are apparent, the process is as follows.

Materials needed:

1. Assortment of flute pads (bladder)
2. Paper flute washers or shims
3. Small screwdriver
4. Pad slick
5. Alcohol burner
6. Feeler gauge
7. Spring hook

Procedure:

1. Remove the key from the body of the instrument, noting the position it must take when replaced and the tension position of all springs as they are unhooked.
2. Almost all pads are held in place by a screw and a flat metal washer; these are next unscrewed and removed from the cup.
3. Carefully remove the old pad so that the washer(s) under the pad can be left in place. It may be noted that there will be more than

one washer and in some instances small pieces placed at strategic places within the cup. If the same thickness of pad can be used as the new replacement, these washers can be left as they are found. If the new pad is of a different thickness, then remove any sections or pieces of the paper washers, leaving at least one or two whole ones in the cup.

4. Select a pad that fits snugly in the cup, fit it into place, and secure it with the flat, metal washer and screw.

5. As the screw is tightened, you will notice several wrinkles will appear in the surface of the pad. These can be removed by dampening the pad with a damp cloth or simply wetting the pad with the lower lip. Take the pad slick, at the same time, heat it lightly over the alcohol burner, and slide it over the surface of the pad—this will iron out all wrinkles.

6. Secure the key back onto the instrument. Using very light finger pressure and the feeler gauge, test around the complete circumference of the pad.

7. If there is an even "drag" in all areas proceed to step #9. If not, note where there is no "drag" from the feeler gauge and remove the key from the instrument once more.

8. Remove the pad, cut a small wedge from one of the paper washers large enough to cover the area which produced no "drag" from the feeler gauge, and set it in the precise place. Replace the pad and redo steps 5 through 7. Retest with the feeler gauge until there is even pressure around the entire rim of the key. If the leak (no "drag") is along the front of the key it can be caused by too many washers in the cup. If the leak is along the back of the key it can be that there are not enough full washers in the cup.

9. Moisten the pad with a damp cloth or with the use of a pipe cleaner and water. Next, clamp or tie the key down and let it dry. This will press a seat into the pad and insure a tight fit.

10. After the pad has dried out and the seat impressed into the pad, adjust the key to other keys it may be aligned with (see Plate XVI flute adjustment).

The pads of the B♮ key and the two trill keys, however, which are located near the head of the flute,

are ordinary pads and can be replaced in an emergency in the following manner.

Materials needed:
1. Tube of liquid cement
2. Size 11½ flute pads
3. Prick punch
4. Pipe cleaner

Procedure:
1. Raise the key and clean out the pad cup. The key does not need to be taken off the instrument.
2. Prick a hole in the edge of the pad with the punch. This will provide a release valve for

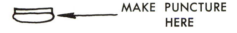

MAKE PUNCTURE HERE

Figure 10.1

any moisture that collects during its use. Failure to do this will result in pads actually blowing up like balloons from the moisture trapped inside the bladder skin.

3. Insert the needle (prick punch) into the side of the cardboard washer on the back of the pad. This will aid in handling the pad as it is put into the cup.

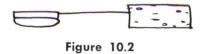

Figure 10.2

4. Place a small amount of liquid cement into the pad cup.
5. Set the pad in place and withdraw the prick punch.
6. Press the key down to set the pad.
7. Dip the pipe cleaner in water and moisten the skin of the pad.
8. Tie the key down and allow it to stand for about an hour or so until the cement dries.

Although the use of liquid pad cement is quite slow, it is the easiest way for the student or layman. However, a much quicker way is to use French pad cement and follow the same procedure as that used for replacing clarinet pads (see page 57, Pad Replacing).

PLATE XVI—FLUTE ADJUSTMENT DIAGRAM

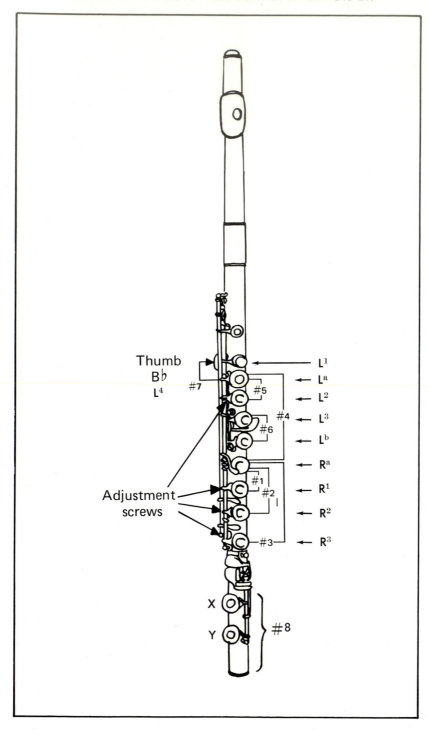

For emergency cases, the pads on a piccolo can be replaced in the same manner as the foregoing. However, because of the miniature key mechanism and close tolerance, any work on the piccolo is best left to a skilled repairman.

C. Testing and Adjusting for Leaks

Materials needed:

1. Feeler gauge
2. Small screwdriver
3. Duckbilled or smooth-jawed pliers

Procedure: (Use with Plate XVI)

1. Insert feeler gauge under key R^a, depress R^1 and withdraw the gauge. A heavy drag on the gauge should be felt.
   a. If no drag is apparent, locate the small adjustment screw which connects these two keys (R^a and R^1) and turn about a quarter-turn (clockwise). Recheck until a good even drag is felt with the feeler gauge.
   b. Insert the feeler gauge under key R^1, depress the key and check for a drag. If little or none is evident, the adjustment screw which controls R^a and R^1 has been turned too far and must be backed off slightly.
   c. Repeat the use of the feeler gauge under first R^a then R^1 to make certain that both keys have an even drag as the gauge is removed.
2. Repeat the same procedure by placing the feeler gauge again under R^a, but working now with this key (R^a) and R^2. Make any adjustments and be certain that both R^a and R^2 seat well as a unit.
3. Repeat the same procedure as above with R^a and R^3.
4. Depress R^1 and notice that not only is the R^a key lowered, but also L^a. Place the feeler gauge under L^a and withdraw to determine the amount of a drag on the gauge. If little or none

exists, the adjustment must be made by bending the bridge key up or down.

Once the L^a key is seating firmly, recheck R^a and R^1. All three keys should work and seat as a unit.

5. Place the gauge under L^a, depress L^2, and withdraw the gauge to determine the seating condition of this key. The adjustment can again be made by working with the small adjustment screw provided.
6. Place the gauge under L^b, depress L^3, and withdraw the gauge noting the amount or absence of drag. If there is little or no drag here, place a pad slick or table knife blade under the L^3 key and gently bend the L^b key down. Recheck.
   a. With the gauge, check to make certain the key has not been bent too far and holds the L^3 key up. If this does occur, place the pad slick under L^b and gently bend the L^3 down.
   b. Recheck both keys to make certain they seat well and as a unit.
7. Place the feeler gauge under the L^a key and depress both thumb keys, withdraw the gauge to determine the drag. If any adjusting needs to be made, the small lever key, which connects the thumb keys to L^a, must be bent.

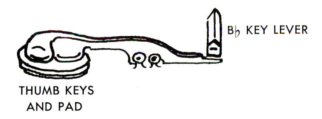

B♭ KEY LEVER

THUMB KEYS
AND PAD

Figure 10.4

Recheck after the lever is bent to see that the key (L^a) seats well, then recheck (using the feeler gauge) to make certain the lever has not been bent too far and the thumb pad is not seating.

8. Place the feeler gauge alternately under keys X and Y and depress the low C key. Both keys should work together as a unit and produce equal drags on the gauge. If an adjustment is necessary, the small bar that connects the two key spatulas must be bent up or down.

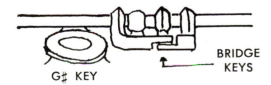

G♯ KEY

BRIDGE
KEYS

Figure 10.3

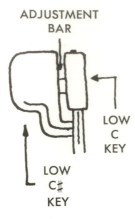

ADJUSTMENT
BAR

LOW
C
KEY

LOW
C#
KEY

Figure 10.5

Assuming that all pads seat independently and barring any other obvious causes, such as broken springs and bent keys, this process of adjusting should eliminate the many common problems unique to the instrument.

Another possible cause for a hard-blowing instrument is an ill-fitting tuning cork in the head joint. This can be tested by sealing the blow hole with the thumb or hand and blowing smoke into the open end. If the smoke seeps out of the other end the tuning cork is not fitting properly. This can be remedied (other than by replacing it) by using one of two methods. The first is to screw down the top washer on the tuning cork, thus causing the cork to bulge.

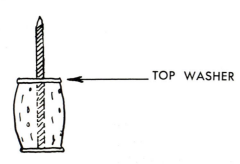

TOP WASHER

Figure 10.6

The other method is to coat the cork with cork grease and rotate it over a flame. This process also will cause the cork to swell.

One other possible reason for a leak in the flute is obviously a bent key. This naturally is also a job for a skilled repairman. It is well in this case to have the entire flute checked for if there has been an accident severe enough to bend a key it is likely that other mechanisms also are out of adjustment.

D. Key Recorking

Corks are cemented on the keys for two reasons: to eliminate noise and for adjustment purposes. Regardless of which factor is involved, if a cork breaks off a key, the outcome is certain to impair the playing ability of the instrument in some way or other. Almost all corks on the flute are very small and located on keys which are difficult to remove from the body of the instrument. For this reason all key corking on the flute should be done with liquid cement. The steps to replace a cork on a key follow.

Materials needed:

1. Tube of liquid cement or contact cement
2. Pieces of cork 1/16″ thick. This thickness of cork is the one used most extensively on the instrument; if a thinner piece is needed it can be cut down after it is cemented to the key.
3. Razor blade
4. Prick punch
5. Small strip of fine sandpaper

Procedure:

1. From the sheet of cork cut a piece a little larger than desired.
2. Stick the prick punch into the edge of the cork.
3. Smear a small dab of liquid cement on the cork.

   If contact cement is used it must be placed on the cork and on the key. Then observe the directions on the container for drying time.

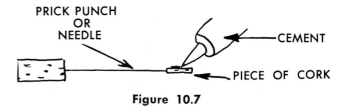

PRICK PUNCH
OR
NEEDLE

CEMENT

PIECE OF CORK

Figure 10.7

4. Work the cork in place, press the key down onto the cork and withdraw the prick punch. Do not press the key down so hard as to squeeze out the cement. The cement will hold the cork in place; the key need not be held down.
5. The cork can be trimmed if necessary after the cement is thoroughly dry; however it is best to leave it alone if it is serving its purpose.

6. Check the height of the key; the cork may have to be thinned out in order to allow the key to have the proper clearance above the tone hole. If some cork must be removed, it can be taken off by placing the thin strip of sandpaper, grit side up, under the cork and slowly withdrawing it.

III. CLEANING

A. Head Joint

The head joint may be cleaned in the following manner.

Materials needed:

1. Tuning rod
2. Cork grease, tallow, or paraffin
3. A basin of warm, soapy water
4. Soft cloth

Procedure:

1. Unscrew the tuning button and remove it.
2. With the tuning rod push the tuning cork down and out of the head joint. Since the bore of the head joint is conical, no attempt

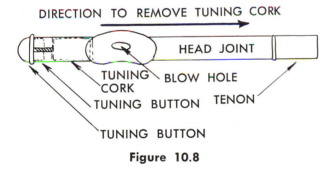

Figure 10.8

should be made to push the cork through the top of the joint.

3. Wash the head joint thoroughly in warm, soapy water, rinse, and wipe it dry.
4. With a bit of denatured alcohol or petroleum jelly, clean the tuning cork, then apply a thin fresh coat of cork grease, tallow, or paraffin.
5. Insert the tuning cork in the bottom end of the head joint and, using the tuning rod, push it into place.
6. The tuning rod that comes with the flute has a mark of 1/2 to 3/4 of an inch from the end.

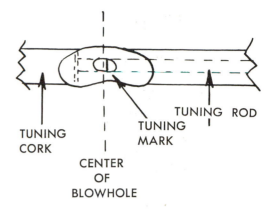

Figure 10.9

The tuning cork should be pushed up into the head joint until this mark appears near the center of the blow hole.

7. The tuning button is next screwed on and the tuning cork pulled up so that the mark on the tuning rod is exactly in the center of the blow hole. This tunes the octaves of the instrument. If a tuning rod is not available one can be made from a wooden stick. The tuning mark is made approximately 17 mm from the

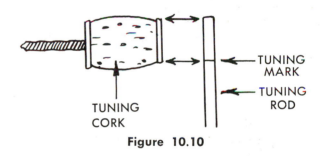

Figure 10.10

end. To be exact, the mark should be the same distance from the tip of the stick as the diameter of the tuning cork's lower washer.

8. Once the cork is set it should not be tampered with.

B. Pads

Flute pads often stick to the tone holes. This is caused by a collection of dirt, saliva, and grease on the pad. The pad can be cleaned in either of two ways.

1. Use a pipe cleaner dampened with benzine or carbon tetrachloride (alcohol may be used but

too much will dry the skin out) to wipe the pad clean.

2. Dampen a thin, clean piece of cloth with either of these liquids, slide it between the pad and the tone hole, gently depress the key and withdraw the cloth.

C. Body

It is very necessary that the instrument be swabbed out after each playing; the tuning rod that comes with the instrument usually is designed so that it can be used for this purpose. When using the rod, care must be taken to see that the cloth covers the entire rod including the tip. This prevents any chance of scratching the bore of the instrument. Silk is recommended over other fabrics because it will not leave lint in the bore. The cloth used should be long enough so that one end can be held in the hand. This will prevent it from bunching up and getting jammed in the bore. The swab should not be left in the case with the instrument. The wet swabs kept within a tight case can provide enough moisture to cause the steel key rods of the mechanism to rust.

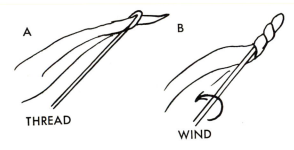

Figure 10.11

IV. RUSTED PIVOT RODS

The presence of moisture within or its proximity to the instrument is a constant hazard to the operation of the key mechanism. The first area to be affected will be the steel rods which serve as pivot rods to almost all keys on the flute, especially key assemblages L^a, L^2, and R^a, R^1-3^a.

These sections of keys have a light spring action, and any presence of corrosion on the pivot rods will show up in the form of one or two sluggish keys.

If this occurs, the key assemblage must be removed from the instrument, cleaned, oiled, and replaced.

Materials needed:

1. Spring hook
2. Small screwdriver
3. Small wire cutters
4. Piece of fine emery paper
5. Key oil
6. Several pipe cleaners

Procedure:

1. Remove all springs connected to the key assemblage.
2. Remove the section from the body of the instrument. On the rod (tube) which connects the various individual keys will be noted several steel wedge pins. These must be removed in order to slide the keys off from the steel pivot rod.
3. With the wire cutter, grasp the wedge pin as close to the rod as possible and pry upwards.

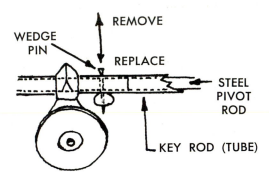

Figure 10.12

Do not put pressure against the key rod!

4. Remove the wedge pin, place it in a safe place, and slide the key off from the main stock.
5. Proceed in this manner until all keys have been removed from the steel pivot rod. Be certain to keep all pins, rods, and keys in exact order!

NOTE: The delicacy of the flute's key mechanism is one that warrants extreme respect. If at any moment, in this process, the failure of removing a wedge pin is a problem, stop and seek the help of a skilled repairman.

6. Using the piece of emery paper, remove the corrosive material from the steel rod. Use light strokes and continually replace the affected key to check its action. Be careful not to re-

move any excess metal which will allow "play" between the steel rod and the key.

7. Once the action of the key is entirely free, run an oil-coated pipe cleaner through the key rod to make sure it is free of any abrasive matter.

8. Replace all keys, rods, and wedge pins in the reverse order as they were disassembled.

NOTE: In replacing the wedge, the hole in the key rod (tube) must align with the matching hole in the steel pivot rod. The wedge pin is then inserted and forced into place.

9. Replace the key assemblage on to the instrument and hook up all springs.
10. Check the action of each key independently.

V. SPECIAL TIPS

Two rather annoying problems seem prevelant with the key mechanism of the flute. With a minimum attention and care both can be alleviated.

1. The spatula of the G♯ key, which extends from the body of the instrument, is frequently bent due to careless handling or assembling. The basic position of the flute in its case also leaves this area of the key exposed and susceptible to damage should the case be dropped or jolted. Either of these incidents can result in a leaking key and difficulty in the playing ability of the instrument.

2. Previous mention has been made in the "General" section of the woodwinds concerning loose rods or pivot screws. Two areas on the flute seem to cause problems in this respect.

The first is the rod which holds the G♯ key. Often this rod, because of the continued action of the keys, will back out and hamper the action of keys L^3 and L^b.

The second area of concern is the small pivot rod which holds the roller bar onto the low C key (located on the foot joint). This, if it works itself out, binds and restricts the action of the E♭ key.

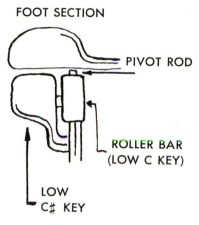

Figure 10.13

Both of these areas should be inspected periodically, and if the problem is apparent, an immediate repair should be made (see p. 101, procedure #8).

VI. INSTRUMENT INSPECTION CHECK SHEET

Flute

Instrument. . . . .   Serial Number.   Make. . . . .

School. . . . .   Private. . . . .   School or Manufacturer's Number . . . .

Finish. . . . .   Other Notations . . . .

	Needs	
O.K.	Attention	

HEAD JOINT

1. Is the tuning button on tight?
2. Does the head joint have a protector cap over the tenon?
3. Is the head joint dented or ovaled?
4. Does the head joint fit securely into the body without any loose play?
5. (Other comments)

BODY AND FOOT JOINT

1. Is the body or foot joint dented or bent?
2. Does the body have a protector cap over the tenon?
3. Are there any broken posts?
4. Are any of the tone holes dented or bent?
5. Does the foot joint fit securely into the body without any loose play?
6.

KEY MECHANISM

1. Are any parts of the key mechanism bent or broken?
2. Are there any loose keys?
3. Are there any pivot screws or key rods missing?
4. Do all keys operate freely and easily?
5. Is the key system overly noisy (due to missing corks or lack of oil)?
6.

PADS

1. Are there any loose or missing pads?
2. Are there any pads in bad condition (torn, hard or brittle, seating improperly, sticking)?
3. Are any of the metal pad washers missing?
4.

CASE

1. Does the case need repair (hinges, locks, or handle)?
2. Does the instrument fit securely in the case?
3. Are there any accessories lying loose in the case which can damage the instrument?
4. Is there a tuning rod in the case?
5.

OTHER COMMENTS

Date . . . .

(signature)

VII. CLASS PROJECT SHEET

Flute

A. Know the names of the various parts of the instrument.

B. Be able to perform the following operations using the correct procedures, techniques, and tools.

    1. Eliminate a leak in one of the keys by:

        a. reseating the pad
        b. adjusting the mechanism

    2. Remedy an ill-fitting tuning cork by:

        a. tightening its top washer
        b. using cork grease and heat

    3. Replace a missing cork on one of the keys

C. Demonstrate the correct methods and procedures for the following operations.

    1. Assemble and disassemble the flute
    2. Test the instrument for leaks
    3. Clean the head joint and tuning cork
    4. Swab out the instrument
    5. Oil the key mechanism
    6. Clean a sticky pad
    7. Adjust the tuning cork in the head joint

D. General.

Be able to give instructions on the daily care and maintenance of the flute with emphasis on eliminating the common errors or bad habits which lead to the need for repair work.

unit three

PERCUSSION INSTRUMENTS

Chapter 11

PERCUSSION INSTRUMENTS

PLATE XVII—SNARE DRUM

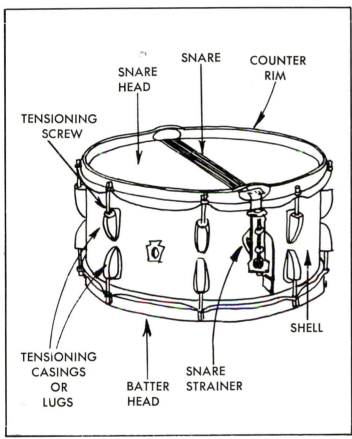

PLATE XVIII—TIMPANI

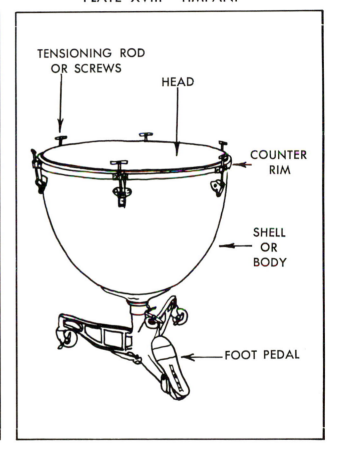

TOOLS AND ACCESSORIES FOR THE REPAIR AND MAINTENANCE OF PERCUSSION INSTRUMENTS

TOOLS

Tablespoon (smooth, rounded end) for use as a tucking tool
Drum key
Large screwdriver
Pair of pliers

ACCESSORIES

Petroleum jelly
Machine oil
Stick of lanolin wax
Bar of paraffin
Strips of linen sheeting, flannel, or felt
Vinegar
Art gum eraser
Shell cleaner and preservative
1. Bowling alley wax
2. Scouring powder
3. Glass wax
Fine emery paper

Percussion instruments are the most neglected members of the musical family when it comes to care and maintenance. Attention rarely is given to the instruments until something either breaks and/or fails to function. Most of the time simple care and periodic checking will eliminate costly repairs. The majority of the information that follows, therefore, is presented with this in mind.

I. THE HEADS

A. Snare and Bass Drums

The most important and delicate section of the drum is, naturally, the head. Therefore, the majority of the care and checking should be undertaken to protect and lengthen the life of this item. Rarely does a head break because of old age and wear. More often than not it is due to carelessness in playing and neglect in care and maintenance.

To begin with, time and money can be saved if the best head available is purchased.

1. Ordering New Heads

When ordering new heads the following facts should be stated:

1. Indicate whether a batter or snare head is desired.
2. Include the make (manufacturer) of the drum for which the head is intended.
3. State size of the head. If it is unknown the diameter of the inside of the old hoop can be measured. If the hoop is not available, the outside diameter of the shell can be measured. Caution should be taken to check first to see that the shell is not warped, thus producing an inaccurate measurement. The most popular size heads are 14, 15, and 16 inch.
4. If desired, the thickness of the head may also be requested. A thin head gives a crisper sound (projects more) but is more easily broken. A thick head is much more durable, but produces a duller sound.
5. Specify whether plastic or calfskin is desired.

NOTE: Though some percussionists prefer the calfskin head for its purity of sound, the advantages of plastic greatly outweigh this one factor.

Calfskin heads are difficult to tune, replace, clean, and maintain; the latter due primarily to the effects of humidity or the lack of it. Plastic heads, on the other hand, require little attention, are made more durable, can be easily cleaned and are rarely affected by moisture.

B. Timpani

1. Ordering New Heads

1. State size of head and size of kettle. If neither of these is known the inside of the old hoop can be measured. If the hoop is not available, the outside diameter of the kettle can be measured. The four most popular sizes are: 30 in., 28 in., 25 in., and 23 in.
2. Include the make (manufacturer) of the drum for which the head is intended.
3. Specify whether plastic or calfskin is desired.

If a calfskin head arrives warped out of shape, it should be returned to the company. It can, however, be straightened by dampening the skin on both sides to within one inch of the edge, placing it on a retainer or drum and allowing it to dry. This usually will straighten it out, though on occasions an overly-warped head should be returned as there are chances it may split in the straightening process. It is wise to keep one or two heads on hand for emergencies. Calfskin heads should be kept on a "head retainer" to prevent warping.

II. TUCKING

A. Snare and Bass Drums

As before stated, the plastic head has made the calfskin head almost obsolete. However, for those few who retain this vestige of the past, the following process of retucking a head is given. It should be noted that these steps can also be followed for replacing skin heads on other instruments of the membranophone family (conga drums and bongos).

Material needed:

Head tucking tool or spoon with smooth rounded handle.

Procedure:

1. For metal hoops, select a head which is approximately five inches larger in diameter than the hoop. If a wooden hoop is used, the head need only be four inches larger. In some in-

stances, because of variances in hoops, the head may have to be trimmed. If this is necessary, be sure to use a sharp pair of scissors and trim evenly around the entire head.

2. Soak the head in clean, room-temperature water until it is soft and pliable. Snare drumheads should be soaked for approximately 30 minutes and bass drumheads for at least 45 minutes. The basin in which the heads are soaked must be large enough so that the heads will not be crushed or folded but can lie relatively flat.

3. Remove the head from the water and place it hair side down on a clean, flat surface. The hair, or beating side, is that side which has the trademark or brand name imprinted upon it.

4. Smooth out all wrinkles and press out all air bubbles so that the head is completely flat. Also wipe away any excess water.

5. Place the hoop directly in the center of the head. If the hoop has one side flat and the other rounded, the flat side should be face down.

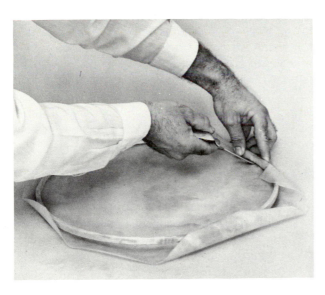

Figure 11.1

6. Using the smooth, rounded end of a tablespoon, which can substitute for a tucking tool, tuck about two inches of the head under a section of the hoop. Be sure it is well under and holds firmly.
(Because of the natural ability of the flesh head to adhere to a wooden hoop it is neces-

sary only to tuck the head over and under the hoop. However, when using a metal hoop the head should be tucked over, under and up the backside.)

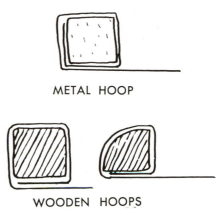

METAL HOOP

WOODEN HOOPS

Figure 11.2

7. Repeat this operation on the side directly opposite. When tucking a snare head do not stretch the head tight, but leave plenty of slack in the middle. If it is a batter head all the slack should be taken up.

8. Repeat the tucking process around the entire hoop in the following order.

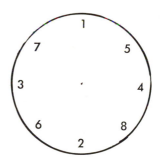

Figure 11.3

9. After all the tucks are in place, work clockwise around the hoop and tuck the remaining portions of the head. It will be necessary periodically to smooth out any lumps, wrinkles, or pleats which occur. This can be done using the backside of the spoon's handle.

10. Place the newly-tucked head back on the shell to dry. To prevent the head from warping,

replace the hoop and screw the rods in using only enough pressure to hold the hoop on. In the case of a bass drum the head is pulled down about one-half of an inch.

11. Set the drum in a cool dry place for approximately eight to ten hours for drying.

B. Timpani

1. Select a head which is approximately six inches larger in diameter than the hoop. In some instances, because of variances in hoops, the head may have to be trimmed. If this is necessary, be sure to use a sharp pair of scissors and trim evenly around the entire head.

2. Soak the head in clean, room-temperature water until it is soft and pliable. This will take about forty-five minutes to an hour. The basin in which the head is soaked must be large enough so that the head will not be crushed or folded, but can lie relatively flat.

3. When the soaked head is laid out on a table ready to be tucked, a great deal of slack must be left in the middle. This can be accomplished by placing an object such as a bowl (about six to eight inches in diameter and four to five inches deep) under the head in the center.

4. Owing to the fact that the timpani hoops are metal, care must be taken to tuck completely around and up the backside of the hoop (see Fig. 11.2, page 113).

5. Tuck in the same order as with the snare head.

6. When the head is completely tucked, place it back on the shell without the counter hoop or snares. Cover the head with a towel or newspaper so that the head will dry evenly and slowly for approximately ten to twelve hours.

7. After this period of time the head will be dry and quite taut. Remove it and, using a damp cloth or sponge, dampen the center of the head up to about one inch from the edge. Place it back on the shell together with the counter hoop and screws. Apply tension to the screws evenly until a one-half inch collar is produced (see Fig. 11.4).

8. Re-cover the head with the towel or newspaper and allow it to dry for at least 24 hours.

III. TENSIONING

A. Snare Drum

As a common rule the tension on a snare drum should remain untouched. There are, however, two exceptions to this rule. One is if the drum has been subjected to a damp atmosphere and the head (calfskin) has been tightened to take up the slack. A mental note should be kept of how many turns were required to pull the head up. When the drum is put away the tension must be returned to its original state. The second exception is if the drum is to be stored for several days or weeks. The head should then be loosened slightly; approximately one full turn of each screw is sufficient. These exceptions should be disregarded if plastic heads are used since humidity, or lack of it, has no effect on them.

In order to have a uniform sounding snare drum section, it is necessary that the timbre of the instruments be as closely alike as possible. If the drums are matched for style and size, if all the sticks used in the section are alike, if the same type of snare is used on all the drums, if care is taken to purchase a good quality head, and if the same brand is used at all times on all the drums, this problem can be minimized. However, the uniformity is destroyed if the drums are tensioned incorrectly. No effort should be made to get a specific pitch, but rather to get a definite timbre. This can be accomplished only if the drum has separate tensioning for each head. The desired result is a crisp, staccato tone with a minimum of ring for carrying power. The following steps should be taken for correct tensioning.

1. Test the batter head first by pushing down on the center of the head with the thumb. There should be only a slight depression or "give." If there is too much, tighten the head up; if there is very little or none, loosen the head slightly.

2. Throw off the snares and, with a drumstick, tap the head in front of each tensioning rod about two inches in. The tones produced should be equal in pitch and timbre. If they are not, tighten or loosen each rod until all the tones are uniform.

3. Turn the drum over and repeat the same operation with the snare head. Remember, however, that the snare head should have less tension than the batter head so that it can vibrate freely against the snares.

4. Make sure the snare, when thrown on, lies flat, even, and well against the head. If it does not, make the necessary adjustments with the snare strainer. (See Plate XVII and refer also to the section on "Snares" in this chapter.)

Uniformity also can be destroyed if one of the drums develops a "ring" or "tubby" sound. Considering first the "ring" in a drum, the following steps should be taken to eliminate it.

1. Owing to the fact that this is prevalent in a cheap drum, rule this factor out immediately by making sure you have an instrument of good quality.
2. See that the tension is even at all points around the head.
3. Rule out a defective head by trying a new one.
4. If plastic snare and batter heads are used, a ringing sound is a common ailment even with a good quality drum. The "ring" can be eliminated by stretching a two-inch band of linen sheeting flannel, or felt, across the diameter of the shell underneath the head. Two pieces of cloth crisscrossed under the head can be used to eliminate even an unusually loud "ring."

If a drum develops a "tubby" sound, one of the following actions should be taken to eliminate it.

1. Check the tension on both heads and make sure they are up.
2. Check the snares to make sure they are not worn (see the section on snares), that they are tight, and that all the strands are flat and flush against the head.
3. The damper or muffler on a good quality drum is used to govern the timbre of the head. This, if too tight, will produce a "tubby" sound; the procedure then is simply to loosen it.
4. Too much cloth has been used as a dampening device (#4 preceding).
5. If neither of these actions eliminates the problem, a new head should be tried. Flaws in a drumhead are possible and are overlooked by even some of the best companies.

B. Bass Drum

To assure a good tone the batter head should be kept slightly tighter than the opposite side. This prevents "kickback" or "bark." For a uniform tone, and to prevent "dead spots" in the head, the tension

must be even at all points around the rim. This can be checked by tapping around the rim at the point of each tightening screw; the tone at each of these points must be alike in pitch and timbre. It is controlled by loosening or tightening the screws.

If the bass drum is used in damp or rainy weather it must be treated like the snare drum; that is, tightened while in use and then loosened when put away. If it is to be stored for a considerable length of time, the tension on both heads should be lowered about one full turn of each screw and the entire drum covered with a cloth or newspaper to prevent dust from collecting on it. After each use, it is well to apply about a half a turn to each of the tensioning rods. Bass drums are played with a little less tension on the heads, and if they are set aside in this manner the head can shrink and the collar will be lost.

C. Timpani

The greatest concern with timpani heads is that of maintaining a collar. The collar is that portion of the head which extends over the rim of the shell to the counter hoop.

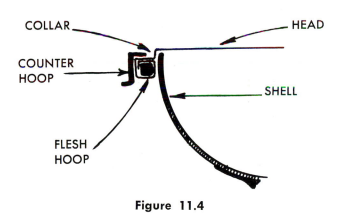

Figure 11.4

If the collar is lost on a head it is impossible to attain the lower note on the instrument. To prevent such a mishap, the timpani should first be kept in a room in which there are no sudden or considerable changes in humidity or temperature. Secondly, the

1. Some percussionists prefer NOT to have a specific pitch to the bass drum and therefore tension the tightening screws unevenly.
2. Note that on some of the drums the tone is pulled a half to a full tone above the highest playing pitch.

heads always should be tightened when the instruments are not in use. Standard procedure is to bring the heads up to their[2] highest pitch; that is, 32 in. G, 30 in. B, 28 in. D, 25 in. F, 24 in. A, and 23 in. G♯. This tensioning process assures an adequate collar when the instruments are used.

If the collar is lost, the following steps should be followed to correct the problem (skin heads).

1. Loosen all screws and remove the counter hoop (see Plate XVIII).
2. With a damp cloth or sponge, moisten the head *evenly* on both sides two or three times within a half hour until the head becomes soft and pliable. Do not dampen the head closer than one inch from the hoop.
3. Replace the counter hoop and apply tension on all the screws until a 3/8- to 1/2-inch collar is produced.
4. In this condition put the instrument away and allow it to dry very slowly. To retard the drying process, cover the head with clean paper or a large damp cloth.

When the correct amount of collar is attained and the head has completely dried, the timpani must be retuned. As contrasted with the snare and bass drum, the timpani must produce definite pitches. The procedure for tuning is standard for all sizes of kettles. The following procedure uses a 28-inch size.

1. Release all tension produced by the hand screws and place the pedal in low position.
2. With the palm of the hand press the head down in the center to make sure it is loose and not sticking to the rim of the shell.
3. Reapply tension by turning the hand screws in pairs, 1 and 4, 2 and 5, 3 and 6. Do not put more than a half turn on each screw.

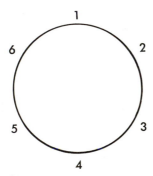

Figure 11.5

4. Continue this operation until low F is produced. It will be necessary occasionally during the retensioning to press the center of the head down to make sure the head is free from the rim of the shell.
5. Using a mallet, tap about two inches in front of each hand screw to make sure the pitch and timbre are equal around the entire head. Raise or lower the pitch by tightening or loosening the head by means of the hand screws.
6. Press the pedal down; a perfect fifth should result, which in this particular case would be C, or higher if desired if plastic heads are used.
7. Test this high tone for pitch and timbre in the same manner used to test the low F; that is, tap in front of each hand screw, compare, and adjust.

Plastic heads are made for the timpani, but are not as satisfactory as calfskin. One reason is the problem of playing a staccato note. With the skin head the tone can be immediately stopped by placing the hand on the head. When this is done with a plastic head the tone is not quite killed and, even worse, the tone that remains changes pitch. The action is similar to placing the finger on a bowed violin string. Another problem arises when only one of the timpani heads is replaced with a plastic head. The tone produced by the plastic head is quite different from that of the skin head. In order to match the set, all the drums must have like heads.

One factor in favor of the plastic heads is their durability and resistance to moisture. Because of this they are ideal for bands which perform out-of-doors concerts.

Because of the expense and delicacy of timpani heads, covers should always be placed over them when the instruments are not in use. It must be remembered that a cheap cover is much less expensive than a timpani head. If nothing else, a suitable cover can be made by cutting a circular piece of cardboard from a large box big enough to cover the entire head.

IV. REPLACING AND CLEANING HEADS

A. Replacing

Whenever a new head is to be replaced on a drum, use the opportunity to inspect the entire instrument thoroughly. All nuts and bolts that appear on the inside or outside of the shell should be checked and tightened. Dust and grease should be removed from the inside of the shell and a careful inspection of the rim should be made. Any small nicks or dents in a metal shell or splinters should be sanded smooth.

When the rim is clean and smooth, a coating of lanolin or paraffin should be rubbed over the entire surface of the rim. This will greatly diminish the wear on the inside (bottom) of the head as it slides back and forth over the rim of the shell.

Inspection of a similar manner should also be given the hoop.

B. Cleaning

A calfskin head may be cleaned with an art gum eraser. The plastic head should be taken off the drum, scrubbed with soap and water—a mild abrasive solution may be used—rinsed, dried, and remounted.

V. THE BODY

A. Snare and Bass Drums

The body and hardware of the drum must also receive periodic checking and care. It is recommended that about twice a year the drum should be completely dismantled.

Metal parts, such as the snare strainer and lugs, should be oiled with a good grade of machine oil. A small dab of petroleum jelly should be rubbed on the threads of the tensioning screws; this not only insures positive action but also prevents rusting.

While the drum is dismantled, all nuts and bolts inside and out should be tightened and any missing ones replaced. Before assembling the instrument, a thin coat of lanolin wax or paraffin should be rubbed on the edges of the shell to minimize wear on the head.

If the shell of the drum is mahogany it can be cleaned and preserved by applying a coat of "bowling alley wax" or a good grade of furniture wax. For pearl finishes glass wax can be used; for a metal shell a kitchen scouring powder works very well.

B. Timpani

Disregarding the new plastic or fiberglass shells, all timpani bodies are polished metal with a lacquer coating. Only a damp cloth or special lacquer polish should be used to clean them. Avoid any polish which has a strong alkali or abrasive in it.

As with the other drums, keep all nuts and screws tightened and grease and oil all moving parts including the casters, footpedals, and lugs.

VI. THE SNARE

A. Gut

Percussionists agree that for indoor concert work alone the gut snare produces the most desired sound; however, when used out-of-doors it lacks volume and carrying power. If the snare is used in damp weather it has a natural tendency to stretch and must be constantly watched and adjusted.

B. Coiled Wire

The coiled wire or Snappy Snare has a great deal of volume and crispness which make it ideal for outside work. Many musicians, however, have found it hard to control for indoor concert work and have had to resort to a lightweight stick in order to arrive at a reasonable balance. If this type of snare is used it is wise to replace it at least every other year. Constant tightening will straighten out the coil in the snare and cause it to lose its tone and crispness. It is also a good policy to loosen the snare strainer after each use. This will take the tension off the coiled wire and allow it to return, somewhat, to its normal position. Frequent checks should also be made on the snare to make certain that no strands have been snagged or bent out of line, thus causing the snare to sound dead. If the wire is badly snagged or bent out of line and is interfering with the vibrations of the other strands, it should be cut out with a pair of wire cutters.

VII. CYMBALS

As with drumheads, it is extremely wise to purchase the best make of cymbals available, then make every effort to lengthen their life.

A. Cleaning

Should the desire arise to have a set of shiny, new-looking cymbals, *never* buff or use a polish that has any abrasive matter in it. The cymbal must be treated as one would care for old silver.

The roughness of a good quality cymbal, according to the manufacturers, is necessary for its tone.

Buffing or rubbing with coarse abrasives smoothes out these rough ridges and diminishes the tone quality of the instrument. The most practical and safe process is to soak the cymbal in vinegar for about half an hour then scrub it gently, using a kitchen cleanser, water, and a soft cloth. The cleaner does have an abrasive in it, but most of the tarnish has been removed by the vinegar so the scrubbing can and should be held to a minimum. If it is impossible to soak the cymbal because of size, it can be placed in a washbasin or bathtub and washed with a vinegar-saturated cloth.

B. Cymbal Grips

Another danger to the life of a good pair of cymbals is the use of fixed wooden handles which are bolted to the bodies of the instrument. These restrict the vibration and, by holding the cymbal in such a rigid position, can create tensions which will cause the cymbal to crack.

Leather straps with lambskin padding are the ideal handles for the cymbals. To secure the strap, proceed as follows.

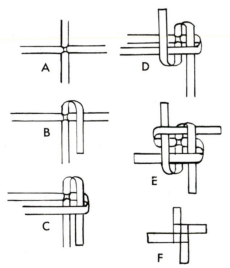

Figure 11.6

C. Cracking

In spite of conscientious care and the insistance for good quality, a cymbal can still become cracked. This is usually the result of some mistreatment or neglect while being played.

Once cracked the true tone of the instrument can never be restored. Therefore, an untrained person should never be allowed to handle them.

If a cymbal does begin to crack, a small hole should immediately be drilled at the extreme end of the crack to halt its progress. A groove should then be sawed or filed along the crack to separate the edges so they do not vibrate together.

Figure 11.7

If the crack is near the edge of the cymbal, it can be ground out (Fig. 11.8a) or off (Fig. 118b) as shown.

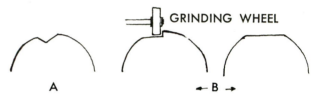

Figure 11.8

Never should an attempt be made to solder, weld, or braze a cymbal. The heat will completely destroy the tone quality of the instrument.

Any crack, no matter how minute, limits the life and use of the cymbal. The tone is not overly distorted, however. It may give continued service as an emergency or rehearsal instrument.

VIII. MALLET INSTRUMENTS

Often the metal resonators on a Glockenspiel fail to respond in an acceptable manner. This can usually be traced directly to the small bolts that hold the bars to the frame. To locate the cause, check to see if:

1. The bolts are too tight and are binding the bar tightly to the frame so it is continually dampened.
2. The small rubber washer is broken or missing causing a metallic vibration as the bar is struck.
3. The small bolt is bent binding the bar. This must be unscrewed and replaced.

Vibraphones, marimbas, xylophones, and chime bars are supported by a cord wound onto a series of guideposts. Often the posts become bent or the cord can become loose or even broken. Should any problems develop with the response of an individual bar or tube, these areas should be checked first.

As a measure of preventive maintenance, all moving parts of the mallet instruments should be periodically oiled with a good grade of machine oil. Burned-out motors or broken drive belts are often the direct result of this neglect.

XI. SPECIAL TIPS

A. Sticks

If the ball ends of the snare sticks are not capped with plastic, they must be inspected continually. Often the wooden tips will become splintered or "roughed-up." In this condition, they can cause serious wear or damage to the head. If the ball end cannot be sanded or smoothed out, they should be discarded or used as a beater for some other percussion instrument.

B. Heads

A problem with plastic heads is their tendency to lose the natural roughness on the batter side. This is especially noticeable when the music calls for a smooth, but audible, brushstroke. The hardness and glasslike surface of the head does not allow the brush to "work" well over the surface and a desired effect is lost. The texture of the plastic head can be restored with the use of a spray product called "Ruff-Coat" and manufactured by one of the leading drum companies.

Many professional trap drummers use a 3″ × 3″ patch of mole skin[1] on the batter head of their bass

1. This can be purchased at a drugstore.

drums where the beater ball continually strikes the head. Not only does this protect the head from wearing but some say it even improves the tone. As the skin patch wears out it can be peeled off and replaced with a new one.

C. Timpani

When adjusting the foot pedal, always keep control of the tension with the foot. The pedal, if suddenly released, can snap against the base and crack itself.

Always keep the tension spring well lubricated to insure a smooth positive action.

Keep the various mallets in a proper storage bag or rack. Never allow the ball end of mallets to lay on an unclean table or pad. The ball of the mallet will pick up dust, dirt, or foreign matter which, if not removed, can damage the head. Watch also for loose threads or exposed ends of the stick.[2]

Tuning devices, though quite accurate when using plastic heads, can never take the place of a good ear and should not be relied upon for accuracy. Their real contribution is realized with the playing of music which has sudden key changes, such as many of our contemporary works.

D. Mallet Instruments

If a cracked or damaged bar is found, remove and send it to the instrument's manufacturer. To insure proper replacement, include the model, make, and serial number of the instrument.

Always cover the bars of the instrument, even if it is only with a sheet of cardboard or a blanket. This will discourage those individuals who cannot resist striking the bars with whatever they happen to have in their hands.

Never store or set anything on top of a mallet instrument.

When moving for any distance, it is wise to dismantle the instrument. When doing so wrap all resonators and the strings of bars in a blanket or quilt.

E. Stands and Cradles

Replace all worn nuts, bolts, or tightening screws and keep all working parts well lubricated. Much damage has been done to a drum or mallet instrument that falls because of an inexpensive screw that is stripped or rusted and not replaced.

F. Cases

When packing, never throw extra sticks, stands, or other gear in with the drum. If possible, use cardboard discs to protect the heads from damage.

Though the fiber case is preferable, cloth bags or even a good cardboard box is cheap insurance against a broken head or damaged snare strainer.

Never store percussion instruments, especially membranophones, in an area that will be subjected to sudden or extreme changes in temperature.

2. See: Arthur Press, *Mallet Repair* (New York, Belwin Mills Publishing Co.), 1971.

G. General

Should the necessity arise to move any or all of the percussion equipment, proper instructions should be given to individuals unfamiliar with the instruments.

Letters or figures painted on bass drumheads do not ordinarily harm the tone. The tone does deteriorate, however, if large areas are painted.

Controversy still reigns as to the correct procedure to be used in tightening down drumheads. One method is to work clockwise around the drum; the other is to cross back and forth to opposite screws. Regardless of which method is used it must be remembered that each screw should not be tightened more than one full turn at a time. This is especially true if the clockwise method is used, as it is very easy to pull the head down farther on the side on which the first screw is tightened.

Before a drum is put away after it has been used in rainy weather, the shell and head should be wiped dry and the hardware wiped with a cloth dampened with machine oil.

X. INSTRUMENT INSPECTION CHECK SHEET

Percussion Instruments (Snares and Bass)

Instrument. . . . .   Serial Number.   Make. . . . .

School. . . . .   Private. . . . .   School or Manufacturer's Number . . . .

Finish. . . . .   Other Notations . . . .

	Needs	
O.K.	Attention	**HEADS**

. . . .   1. Is either the batter or snare head broken?
. . . .   2. Are there any cuts in either head?
. . . .   3. Is the head pulling loose from the flesh hoop in any spots around the hoop?
. . . .   4. Does the head need cleaning?
. . . .   5. Are the counter hoops on evenly?
. . . .   6. Does the drum have a tubby sound or an unusually loud ring?
. . . .   7. Is there proper tension on each head?
. . . .   8. Are the pitch and timbre even on the head in front of each tightening screw?
. . . .   9. Is the snare head being cut on the edges by the snare?*
. . . . 10. (Other comments)

SHELL AND ACCOUTERMENTS

. . . .   1. Are there any lugs (tightening screws) missing?
. . . .   2. Are all the lugs in proper working order?
. . . .   3. Are any of the lugs loose on the shell?
. . . .   4. Is the shell damaged in any way?
. . . .   5. Does the snare strainer work freely and properly?*
. . . .   6.

SNARE*

. . . .   1. Are any of the strands on the snare badly bent or broken?
. . . .   2. Do all the strands lie evenly on the head?
. . . .   3. Does the snare function properly?
. . . .   4. If a wire snare is used, is the coil or spiral still in the strand or has it been stretched out?
. . . .   5.

GENERAL

. . . .   1. Are the drums stored in a place free from extreme heat and humidity?
. . . .   2. Are the pitch and timbre even on all snare drums?*
. . . .   3. Are the drums in cases, cages, or protected in some way from dust and/or damage?*
. . . .   4. Are all stands or cradles in good condition?
. . . .   5. Are all rubber guards on the feet and arms present and in good condition?
. . . .   6.

OTHER COMMENTS

Date . . . .
                                                                  (signature)

*For snare drums only.

XI. INSTRUMENT INSPECTION CHECK SHEET

Percussion Instruments (Timpani)

Size of Drum or Description.. Make...................

School or Manufacturer's Number........................ Other Notations...............................

	Needs	
O.K.	Attention	**HEADS**

....1. Are any of the heads broken?

....2. Are there any cuts in any of the heads?

....3. Is the head pulling loose from the flesh hoop in any spots around the hoop?

....4. Does the head need cleaning?

....5. Are the counter hoops on evenly?

....6. Is there a proper amount of collar on each head (at least a half inch)?

....7. Is there any grating noise present as the head is tightened and loosened?

....8. (Other comments)

SHELL AND ACCOUTERMENTS

....1. Are any of the tightening rods or hand screws missing?

....2. Does the foot pedal mechanism work properly, freely, and without any noise?

....3. Are there any large dents in the shell?

....4. Do the casters move freely and lock properly?

....5.

OTHER COMMENTS

Date ....
                                                                                          (signature)

XII. INSTRUMENT INSPECTION CHECK SHEET

Percussion Instruments (Mallet Instruments)

Instrument. . . . .   Serial Number. . . . .   Make. . . . .

School. . . . .   Private. . . . .   School or Manufacturer's Number . . . .

Finish. . . . .   Other Notations . . . .

. . . . .1.   Are there accumulations of dust or oily deposits on bars or tubes?
. . . . .2.   Are there any bent or broken guideposts?
. . . . .3.   Are the cords broken or badly frayed?
. . . . .4.   Are any of the insulator washers missing or worn?
. . . . .5.   Are any of the bars badly dented, cracked, or splintered?
. . . . .6.   Are all drive belts in good condition?
. . . . 7.   Are all pulleys functioning properly?
. . . . 8.   Does the "on" and "off" switch work properly?
. . . . 9.   Do the casters move freely and lock properly?
. . . . .10.   Is the damper mechanism in good working condition?
. . . . .11.   Are all legs sturdy and well bolted?
. . . . .12.   (Other comments)

OTHER COMMENTS

Date . . . .

(signature)

XIII. INSTRUMENT INSPECTION CHECK SHEET

Percussion Instruments (Accessories)

Size of Drum or Description.................................... Make..................

School or Manufacturer's Number...................... Other Notations...............................

...............................1. Are all mallets clean and stored properly?
...............................2. Are all the heads of the mallets on securely?
...............................3. Do any snare sticks have broken or frayed ends?
...............................4. Are the holding straps on the cymbals broken or badly worn?
...............................5. (Other comments)

OTHER COMMENTS

Date ....
                                                              (signature)

APPENDIXES

APPENDIX A

REPAIR MANUALS AND AIDS

Books and Manuals

Brand, Erick D. *Band Instrument Repairing Manual.* Elkhart, Indiana: Erick D. Brand, 1946.

Kirschner, Frederick. *Encyclopedia of Band Instrument Repair.* New York: Music Trade Review, 1962.

Meyer, R. F. "Peg." *The Band Director's Guide to Instrument Repair.* Port Washington, New York: Alfred Publishing Co., Inc., 1973.

Nilles, Raymond J. *Basic Repair Handbook for Musical Instruments.* Fullerton, California: F. E. Olds & Son, 1959.

Springer, George H. *Maintenance and Repair of Band Instruments.* Boston: Allyn & Bacon, 1970.

Weisshaar, Otto. *Preventive Maintenance of Musical Instruments.* Rockville Centre, New York: Belwin, Inc., 1966.

Filmstrips

The Apprenticeship Series. 738 Lindsay Road, Carnegie, Pennsylvania.

Band Instrument Care (set 10 strips). Educational Audio Visual, Inc., Pleasantville, New York.

APPENDIX B

CARE AND MAINTENANCE PAMPHLETS

Conn Corporation. *How to Care for Your Instrument*. Elkhart, Indiana: C. G. Conn Ltd., 1942.

Hovey, Nilo W. *Selmer Band Manual*. Elkhart, Indiana: H. & A. Selmer, Inc., 1955.

King Musical Instruments. *How to Care for Your Instrument. Instruction Guide for Brass Instruments*. Eastlake, Ohio: King Musical Instruments, Division of the Seeburg Corporation (n.d.).

———. *How to Care for Your Instrument. Instruction Guide for Trombones*. Eastlake, Ohio: King Musical Instruments, Division of the Seeburg Corporation (n.d.).

———. *How to Care for Your Instrument. Instruction Guide for Woodwinds*. Eastlake, Ohio: King Musical Instruments, Division of the Seeburg Corporation (n.d.).

Lehman, Paul R. *Teacher's Guide to the Oboe*. Elkhart, Indiana: H. & A. Selmer, Inc., 1965.

Pascucci, Vito. *Care and Minor Repairs of the Clarinet for Band Directors*. Kenosha, Wisconsin: G. Leblanc Corporation, 1959.

Pence, Homer. *Teacher's Guide to the Bassoon*. Elkhart, Indiana: H. & A. Selmer, Inc., 1963.

Weisshaar, Otto H. *Preventive Maintenance of Musical Instruments*. Rockville Centre, New York: Belwin, Inc., 1966.

APPENDIX C

INSTRUMENT REPAIR SUPPLY HOUSES

Ed Myers Company, 3022 Pacific Street, Omaha, Nebraska 68105

Erick Brand, Elkhart, Indiana 46514

Ferree's Band Instrument Tools and Supplies, 110 Calhoun Street, P. O. Box 259, Battle Creek, Michigan 49016

APPENDIX D

INSTRUMENT REPAIR SCHOOLS*

Ferree's, Box 259, Battle Creek, Michigan 49016

Mr. Wayne Kyle, Director of Vocational Education, Western Tech., 3075 Floyd Blvd., Sioux City, Iowa

Mr. Bob Getzen, Allied Music, Inc., Elkhorn, Wisconsin

Mr. Gary Roth, Spokane Falls Community College, W3410 Fort George Wright Drive, Spokane, Washington 99204

*Many educational institutions offer short courses on the subject. The above listed schools, however, offer a complete course for the training of a professional repairman.

APPENDIX E

REPAIR SHOP JOB DESCRIPTIONS*

Sample No. 1

ALL BRASS overhauls (Nos. 1, 2, 3, and 4) will include cleaning inside and out; new felts, corks, and springs where necessary; valve alignment and adjustment; soldering of loose braces or connections; clean case.

ALL SAX overhauls will include cleaning inside and out, solder loose braces and connections; new key corks; all new high quality pads; new springs where necessary; assembling, oiling, complete adjustment, and testing; clean case.

ALL WOODWIND overhauls include cleaning inside and out; highly polish keys; all new high quality pads; key corks and joint corks; new springs where necessary; tighten loose rings; complete adjustment and testing; clean case.

DEFINITIONS:

Job No. 1—includes above listing under BRASS. This does not include any dent removal, but does include buff and lacquer.

Job No. 2—includes above listing under BRASS or SAX. This is the Econohaul and all large dents are removed, no very small dents, pits, or scratches. This includes buffing and lacquer, replate one mouthpiece.

Job No. 3—includes listing under BRASS. This is removal of all dents, highly polished and lacquered, replate one mouthpiece.

Job No. 4—includes above listing under BRASS. This is silver stripping of silver instruments and complete refinishing to brass as in Job No. 3. Replate one mouthpiece.

Cleaning Woodwinds—includes disassembling entire instrument, cleaning keys and body, reassembling, adjusting, and testing.

Flushing Brasses—includes flushing and cleaning entire instrument inside and out, greasing all slides, oiling and adjusting valves, new corks and felts where necessary.

Please mark all instruments sent for overhaul as Job No. 1, No. 2, No. 3, or No. 4. *Any unmarked instruments will go under Job No. 3.*

Silver-plated instruments not to be stripped will be overhauled under Job No. 2 and will include shine and polish.

All jobs do not include new parts. New parts are an extra charge.

Sample No. 2

Overhauling woodwind instruments consists of disassembling the instrument, cleaning, and sterilizing; highly polished keys; finest pads and corks; and all new cork joints. Every instrument completely adjusted and tested. New parts extra.

*Selected from random published repair price lists.

All jobs do not include any necessary new parts. Parts are governed by the original manufacturer. We will be pleased to forward an estimate of the cost of repairing an instrument for your approval before beginning work, if you so request.

The _____ Music Corporation now offers their modern plating facilities to all shops who are unable to process their own plating. This would include stripping of the old plating, buffing, and replating.

Consists of disassembling the instrument, cleaning, and sterilizing, new corks, felts, pads, springs when necessary. High lustre polish on all brass instruments with baked clear lacquer. Carefully adjusted and tested. Major dents on Job 1 and 2 upon request at a modest charge. One mouthpiece on Job 3 and 4 will be replated at no charge.

Add $_____ to all Selmar Saxophones if they are to be restored to the original "Selmer-Color," and are supplied with original Selmer pads. On the Meinl-Weston, Miratone, and 4 valve tubas, there will be an additional charge. Ask for a quotation.

If possible ship all instruments to us without cases. This cuts down on the damage caused by bouncing and movement in the cases. If you wish to ship by bus or United Parcel then cases are a convenience. We will accept the instruments with or without cases, but through experience we find much less damage without them.

Lacquer is only a temporary finish and is so listed by the National Association of Band Instrument Manufacturers. A lacquer finish therefore cannot be guaranteed. We are, however, using the newest formula Durachem Epoxy oven-baked lacquer for added protection.

Sample No. 3

BRASS
—Our Complete Overhaul Consists of—

1. Lacquer completely removed.
2. Instrument thoroughly cleaned and sterilized.
3. All accessible dents removed.
4. Slides, pistons, and casings polished.
5. All springs, corks, and felts replaced.
6. Valves carefully adjusted.
7. Instrument tested for leaks.
8. Instrument polished and lacquered (two coats Nikolas lacquer).

An additional charge will be made for all work such as repairing or replacing broken or worn parts, removing major dents, refitting valves, and pulling frozen slides.
(If desired, prices will be quoted on above repairs before proceeding).

REEDS—FLUTES
—Our Complete Overhaul Consists of—

1. Removal of all keys, pads, springs, and corks, and, if lacquered, worn finish is stripped.
2. Swedging of all keys to insure good action.
3. Cleaning and sterilizing.
4. Dents removed and posts tightened and aligned.
5. Keys and body polished and color buffed.
6. Lacquered.
7. Assembling—we furnish ALL new pads, corks, felts, and springs where needed.

8. Testing for leaks, intonation, and playing quality.
9. Final coat of lacquer applied.
10. Final testing and adjusting.

Extra charge will be made for sealing or pinning cracks in wood instruments and silver soldering or replacing broken keys. One new cork joint is included in the overhaul price. Other cork joints, if necessary, will be charged for at the rate of $1.00 each.

PAD CHART AND GRAPH*
(Clarinet and Flute)

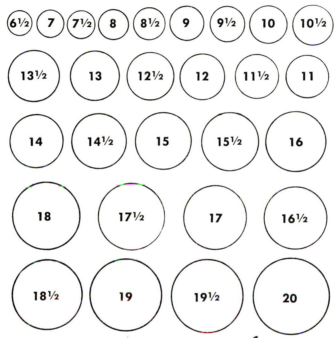

ACTUAL MILLIMETER SIZES OF PADS

Size in 32nd inches	Size in millimeters	Size in 32nd inches	Size in millimeters	Size in 32nd inches	Size in millimeters	Size in 32nd inches	Size in millimeters	Size in 32nd inches	Size in millimeters
9/32	7	25/32	20	41/32	32½	57/32	45	73/32	58
10/32	8	26/32	20½	42/32	33½	58/32	46	74/32	58½
11/32	9	27/32	21½	43/32	34	59/32	47	75/32	59½
12/32	9½	28/32	22	44/32	35	60/32	47½	76/32	60½
13/32	10	29/32	23	45/32	36	61/32	48½	77/32	61
14/32	11	30/32	24	46/32	36½	62/32	49	78/32	62
15/32	12	31/32	24½	47/32	37½	63/32	50	79/32	62½
16/32	12½	32/32	25½	48/32	38	64/32	51	80/32	63½
17/32	13½	33/32	26	49/32	39	65/32	51½	81/32	64½
18/32	14½	34/32	27	50/32	40	66/32	52½	82/32	65
19/32	15	35/32	28	51/32	40½	67/32	53	83/32	66
20/32	16	36/32	28½	52/32	41½	68/32	54	84/32	66½
21/32	16½	37/32	29½	53/32	42	69/32	55	85/32	67½
22/32	17½	38/32	30	54/32	43	70/32	55½	86/32	68½
23/32	18½	39/32	31	55/32	43½	71/32	56½	87/32	69
24/32	19	40/32	32	56/32	44½	72/32	57	88/32	70

*Courtesy Ferree's Band Instrument Tools and Supplies Catalog.